ENDORSEMENTS

"My friend, Nicole Montgomery, has written her first book entitled, *Get Back UP!* It is a great reminder that we can truly overcome those hard moments in life and move forward with wisdom and grace."

—VICTORIA OSTEEN, CO-PASTOR OF LAKEWOOD CHURCH
NEW YORK TIMES BEST SELLING AUTHOR

"*Get Back UP!* is filled with refreshingly honest, spirit-led, timely encouragement. Author Nicole Montgomery, JD MPA, shares relatable, heartwarming examples to navigate life's journey. Her words, woven with wit and wisdom, gently remind us to keep God at the center of it all."

—NORMA L. JARRETT, JD, AUTHOR/NOVELIST-PENGUIN-RANDOMHOUSE

"Read and then read again *Get Back UP!* It's full of the encouragement, Biblical wisdom, and practical steps we all need as we go through the challenges everyone encounters sooner or later. Real life and relatable stories abound so you can see that these principles really work when we experience hard times."

—WANDA GOODE, CRU/LEADERIMPACT

"*Get Back UP!* has evergreen encouragement for nearly every difficult life circumstance. Nicole Montgomery helps us to recognize that no one need face difficulties without God as a partner. She shows us how to walk hand-in-hand with Him through her sage advice and shared personal experiences. This book will be permanently parked on my bedside table. It's a keeper!"

—MELANIE STILES, CHRISTIAN LIFE COACH, AUTHOR, EDITOR

Becky,
May this be a refreshing season for you!

Warm Regards,
Nicole
Psalms 121

Get Back UP!
Overcoming the Hard Moments in Life

Copyright © 2023 by Nicole Montgomery

All rights reserved. No part of this book may be used or reproduced by any means, graphic, electronic, or mechanical, including scanning, photocopying, recording, taping or by any information storage retrieval system without the written permission of the publisher except in the case of brief quotations embodied in critical articles and reviews.

The content within this book is intended to be inspirational. It does not promise any particular guaranteed outcome. The author assumes no responsibility for the reader's interpretations thereof.

You may contact the author at:

Nicole@NicoleMontgomery.com
www.NicoleMontgomery.com
2802 Timmons Lane #27424
Houston, Texas 77227

The views expressed in this work are solely those of the author.

ISBN: 9798393677756

Cover Design and Interior Format: Crystal L Barnes, Better Way Publishing LLC, www.crystal-barnes.com
Cover Image: iStock by Getty Images
Nicole's Photo: Brandon Vos with Stuiod Vos

Scripture quotations marked ESV are taken from the *ESV® Study Bible (The Holy Bible, English Standard Version®)*, Copyright © 2008 by Crossway, a publishing ministry of Good News Publishers. Used by permission. All rights reserved.

Scripture quotations marked KJV are taken from the King James Version. Public Domain.

Scripture quotations marked MSG are taken from The Message, copyright © 1993, 2002, 2018 by Eugene H. Peterson. Used by permission of NavPress. All rights reserved. Represented by Tyndale House Publishers.

Scripture quotations marked NASB are taken from the (NASB®) New American Standard Bible®, Copyright © 1960, 1971, 1977, 1995 by The Lockman Foundation. Used by permission. All rights reserved. Lockman.org.

Scripture quotations marked (NIV) are taken from the Holy Bible, New International Version®, NIV®. Copyright © 1973, 1978, 1984, 2011 by Biblica, Inc.™ Used by permission of Zondervan. All rights reserved worldwide. www.zondervan.com The "NIV" and "New International Version" are trademarks registered in the United States Patent and Trademark Office by Biblica, Inc.™

Scripture taken from the New King James Version®. Copyright © 1982 by Thomas Nelson. Used by permission. All rights reserved.

Scripture quotations marked (NLT) are taken from the Holy Bible, New Living Translation, copyright ©1996, 2004, 2015 by Tyndale House Foundation. Used by permission of Tyndale House Publishers, Carol Stream, Illinois 60188. All rights reserved.

Scripture quotations marked TPT are from The Passion Translation®. Copyright © 2017, 2018, 2020 by Passion & Fire Ministries, Inc. Used by permission. All rights reserved. ThePassionTranslation.com.

DEDICATION

This book is dedicated to all the wonderful people who have sown into my life. I am grateful for their encouragement, love, patience, perseverance, and accountability.

It is such a fallacy to think we arrive by ourselves or because of ourselves. There is this beautiful village that has carried me through some of the toughest moments in my life. And those same people stayed around to celebrate me. Thank you for your love and showing up in my life.

I would like to say a special thank you to my editor, Melanie Stiles, who marched beside me on this long, winding path to publish my first book.

I would like to thank my mother, Rose, who encouraged me every step of the way.

I would like to thank my spiritual mother, Dr. Barbara Guthrie, who counseled, prayed and corrected me in love for over twenty years. Words cannot express how grateful I am to God for giving me such a gift.

I would like to thank my sister Kelli, along with my nephew and niece for listening, supporting and processing with me.

There are so many more who go unnamed, but are truly valued.

With Love,
Nicole

OVERCOMING THE HARD MOMENTS IN LIFE

Nicole Montgomery

TABLE OF CONTENTS

BEFORE WE BEGIN… V
-1-WHEN YOU WANT TO GIVE UP… - 1 -
-2-WHEN YOU ARE AFRAID… - 7 -
-3-WHEN YOU EXPERIENCE A HEALTH CRISIS… - 13 -
-4-WHEN YOU NEED A NEW SELF-IMAGE… - 19 -
-5-WHEN YOUR FAITH IS SHIPWRECKED… - 25 -
-6-WHEN YOU FEEL LOST… - 31 -
-7-WHEN YOU ARE SINGLE LATE IN LIFE… - 37 -
-8-WHEN YOU FEEL FORGOTTEN… - 43 -
-9-WHEN IT'S TIME TO FIGHT… - 49 -
-10-WHEN IT'S TIME FOR A CHANGE… - 55 -
-11-WHEN YOU TAKE STEPS OF FAITH… - 61 -
-12-WHEN YOU ARE TEMPTED TO HATE… - 67 -
-13-WHEN IT IS TIME TO BE BRAVE… - 73 -
-14-WHEN YOU FEEL BETRAYED… - 79 -
-15-WHEN YOU HAVE FAILED… - 85 -
-16-WHEN LIFE IS OVERWHELMING… - 89 -
-17-WHEN YOU WALK ALONE IN YOUR DREAM… - 95 -
-18-WHEN YOU HAVE AN EMOTIONAL WOUND… - 101 -
-19-WHEN IT'S TIME TO REBUILD… - 107 -
-20-WHEN YOU FEEL UNWORTHY… - 113 -
-21-WHEN YOU CHANGE YOUR PERSPECTIVE… - 119 -

GET BACK UP!

-22- WHEN YOU EXPERIENCE TRAUMA…	- 125 -
-23- WHEN YOU NEED A COMEBACK…	- 131 -
-24- WHEN IT'S TIME TO BEGIN AGAIN…	- 137 -
AUTHOR BIO	- 143 -
GET BACK UP! SCRIPTURES	- 144 -

"The Lord makes firm the steps of the one who delights in him; though he may stumble, he will not fall, for the Lord upholds him with His hand."

Psalms 37:23-24 NIV

"Now thanks be to God who always leads us in triumph in Christ, and through us diffuses the fragrance of His knowledge in every place."

2 Corinthians 2:14 NKJV

"Is anything too hard for the Lord? I will return to you at the appointed time next year, and Sarah will have a son."

Genesis 18:14 NIV

BEFORE WE BEGIN...

Do you need a comeback? If you are like me, then you probably love a good comeback story, especially since there is often pain, disappointment and failures that precede the need for a divine return. Many of us start off with high hopes and visions of grandeur. Yet, life can provide a rude awakening with the realization that accomplishing our goals and dreams will not be as easy as we expect. In fact, they can be extremely difficult.

I have always had a hard time reconciling life's struggles with faith. Let me just confess right now that if I'm not watchful, I can be overly optimistic. Even Jesus tells us in John 16:33 NLT, "I have told you all this so that you may have peace in me. Here on earth you will have many trials and sorrows. But take heart, because I have overcome the world." Yet, as a young Believer, I erroneously thought with God's grace and enablement, I could do anything and would not experience true hardship. I guess I also thought that I would be spared difficulty and suffering if I believed with faith. I'm not suggesting that I expected to plow through a door, leap over a tall building or considered God my sugar daddy. I just didn't fully appreciate that we must partner with God to reach our dreams and overcome challenges in life. We don't get to wish problems away or have them disappear with the snap of our fingers. Instead, if we fall down, then we have to <u>Get Back UP!</u> With our legs. With our hands. With our **spirit-led** gumption. It really is that simple.

At the same time, God is there with resources to help us rise from the ashes. He is also there to give direction when we lose our way or when we are afraid. However, in the end, it's our journey. We grow in faith and trust in our Heavenly Father's faithfulness and love for us.

Our trust muscle is incredibly important because we cannot predict what will happen in life. Just like the COVID pandemic took the world by surprise, this life will provide unexpected challenges that are beyond our control. There is a degree of uncertainty in every daily step; and unquestionably, there are some seasons that are harder than others. Yet, our firm foundation and certainty comes from knowing the character of our Father God. He is good, merciful, and kind.

May you be inspired, and hopefully a spark of passion be ignited, as you read through these pages. My prayer is that you rise up from the ashes of disappointments, setbacks, and defeats with purpose and trust. In this community of Believers, you will find that you are not alone. And where you stand is not the end, but rather the beginning of something new and beautiful that our Lord God wants to do in your life.

To accomplish our dreams and purpose, we have to be tenacious and have the heart of a champion. So, no matter what circumstance or difficulty we are facing, I'm here to announce that it is time for you to Get Back UP! I believe there is so much more good to come in the future—in spite of the struggles of the past.

Warmest Regards,
Nicole

-1-
WHEN YOU WANT TO GIVE UP...

The reality is that life can throw us curveballs that we did not see coming. Our challenge is to endure setbacks and hardships on the way to making our dreams come true. This will not always be easy. There will be times when we want to give up. It often means persevering through failure, humiliation, and inadequacy.

Actually, it reminds me of the season I first learned to play volleyball. Although it is one of my favorite sports, and I had the pleasure of being all-city at one point, it did not start out that way. In fact, I was an extremely awkward and clumsy seventh grader learning the sport. I was the girl who was always falling down as a youngster and often chosen last for dodgeball and kickball.

Nevertheless, there I was, ready to learn and faithful in daily practice. Yes, positively dedicated during that first season to consistently put out lights in the gym ceiling when I bumped the ball or regularly served the ball into the net. I am not completely sure how I made the second string team. Obviously, the coach saw more in me than I saw in myself—or maybe he needed the additional numbers.

GET BACK UP!

I wish I could tell you that I started to incrementally improve through the season, but I did not get any better. Anyone looking at the situation would say it was hopeless, with no sign of improvement. That first season, I got the chance to say I was part of the team—the part that warmed the bench. I also made many friends and learned a lot about failure. The great news is that I was on a winning team that year. Our varsity team made it to the playoffs, but somehow started to fall apart and eventually lose the first game. While on the brink of losing the second game, along with any hopes of continuing in the tournament, our team coach had an epiphany; and, I suspect a moment of frustration. Coach did a massive substitution by placing the junior varsity team on the court. Moreover, to make matters worse, he placed yours truly as the server.

As soon as I saw the lineup, I rushed over to remind him that I had not served a ball over the net all season in practice. I begged him to take me out of the game, but the buzzer sounded, indicating that it was too late to make any additional changes. There I was at the serving line, knowing that I had failed this same task so many times before. I actually remember having a private mini-meltdown while bouncing the ball to prepare the serve. I never prayed so hard over a ball in my entire life. I knew the Lord wanted me to try, even though I didn't think I could do it. I realize now that it was preparation for the many experiences to come in my life when I would not feel up for the challenge.

As I prepared to serve the ball during that frightful game, I looked at my coach for support, but was only met with a defeated and hopeless expression. No one believed in me at that moment. I knew I was on my own. I silently asked God to be with me and help me because I knew that I could not do it without Him. To my utter surprise, the ball went over the net, barely, as if an angel carried it over. Equally amazing, the other

WHEN YOU WANT TO GIVE UP...

team did not know how to defend my serve. I was ready to celebrate and move on, but they gave me the ball again. In volleyball, you continue serving until you miss. This, of course, shows how much I had absorbed the rules from the previous three months. After serving multiple winning points, my coach was on his feet yelling instructions to the team. The varsity team was shocked, and the crowd was cheering us on. The seventh grade newbies won the game for our school. After a short time out, the school's first team was back on the court for the final game of the match. I do not recall which school won the best two out of three games. Probably because I sat in a daze on the players bench, still numb from what I had just experienced. I served a winning game. I had failed so many times before, but not this time. God rescued me.

As we experience new opportunities in the areas that we have previously failed, we cannot shrink back with fear. We have to believe that God will give us a comeback. I had a really hard season learning to play volleyball. I was embarrassed and humiliated at every practice because I could not hide my lack of coordination and inability to learn the sport.

There were many times that I wanted to quit, give up, and walk away. It seemed like the perfect opportunity for me at first, but then, it got difficult. I was not improving. Yet, I continued to persevere and persist during that difficult time. It was not easy to bear all those months of inadequacy and failure. However, I kept showing up, which is sometimes the most important thing. I was determined to press through believing that God would help me to reach my goal.

Likewise, life can be hard. Everyone will have to tolerate tough situations at some point. There will be moments that we want to give up. We will be uncomfortable, humbled, and even fail at times. Nevertheless, even in failure, we have to push forward. Sometimes, we may not know the end result. These are

GET BACK UP!

the times that we must remind ourselves of Hebrews 12:1-2 ESV, "Therefore, since we are surrounded by so great a cloud of witnesses, let us also lay aside every weight, and sin which clings so closely, and let us run with endurance the race that is set before us, looking to Jesus, the founder and perfecter of our faith, who for the joy that was set before him endured the cross, despising the shame, and is seated at the right hand of the throne of God." I would also add that Jesus is, right now, making intercession for us. I often think about my loved ones in Heaven as part of that cloud of witnesses cheering me on.

I figured that I would probably never be a great volleyball player, but I was wrong. I worked hard during the off-season. I made the varsity team the next school year.

Eventually, I made the all-city team as the number one server. When we persevere through the strenuous moments in life, we learn about faithfulness, resilience, and ourselves. We learn that there is great reward on the other side of the challenge. We don't really need to know how the reward will look. Part of trusting God's faithfulness is believing that we will find it beautiful. In Isaiah 61:3 NIV, we are told that God will "…provide for those who grieve in Zion—to bestow on them a crown of beauty instead of ashes, the oil of joy instead of mourning, and a garment of praise instead of a spirit of despair. They will be called oaks of righteousness, a planting of the Lord for the display of his splendor." Although we do not know God's plan for our lives, we are trusting His love, protection, and faithfulness.

WHEN YOU WANT TO GIVE UP...

PRAYER

Dear Heavenly Father, I pray that You would give my dear friends fortitude and strength to endure the hardships that often come with growth. May they be strengthened and know that with You they will make it to the other side of every hard place. May they have Your grace to bear them up during their most challenging moments. Lord, open their eyes to see the beauty You have for them in this season. In Jesus' Name, amen.

GETTING UP MOMENT

Write out three scriptures that speak victory over your situation.

-2-
WHEN YOU ARE AFRAID...

I would describe myself as moderately adventurous. I love new experiences that are fun and exciting, including traveling outside of the United States. Although I am not the daredevil type, I surprised myself by allowing a good friend to talk me into horseback riding in the Caribbean Sea off the coast of Saint Lucia. Soon I was riding bareback on a horse (for the first time). And in the ocean. The question will always remain whether it was I who was more afraid of drowning or whether the horse feared I would kill him as I yanked and intertwined my fingers in his mane with an incredible force. Our tour guide kept instructing me to relax and just flow with it. *Yeah, easy for him to say.*

The scariest part of my experience was when I could no longer feel the ocean floor beneath the horse. At some point, I unconscientiously decided to let go with the realization that this moment in my life was completely out of my control. There was nothing I could do, but pray. And since my day in the ocean, there have been so many more moments in my life that I felt were beyond me. God has used those moments to remind me that He **is** in control and to trust Him.

GET BACK UP!

I know that I am not alone in the struggle to adjust to life's sometimes unruly predicaments. Whether a personal health scare, a sick loved one, troubles on the job, or a financial crisis, life provides all of us with many opportunities to be afraid. In those unexpected, chaotic situations, we must trust in our all-powerful God to protect us, lead us and see us through. We may not understand what is happening in real-time. We don't always have answers, but the good news is that we belong to a God who does not fail. Our Heavenly Father's solution may not look the way we expect. Just as when the three Hebrew teenagers were thrown into the fiery furnace by King Nebuchadnezzar (Daniel 3:20), we too may have to endure blazing and terrifying trials that would make the strongest knees wobble. However, we can be certain that God is with us in the most challenging circumstances, as He was with Shadrach, Meshach, and Abednego.

With my surrender during that mind-blowing experience, as I was surrounded by water and waves, the most amazing thing happened right before my eyes. The horse began to swim. *Imagine that!* The problem was not the horse, but rather me. The conflict and tension I felt was born out of fear. I could not fully enjoy that moment or live in the adventure because of fear. The Word of God encourages us not to fear in 2 Timothy 1:7 NKJV, "For God has not given us a spirit of fear, but of power and of love and of a sound mind."

I suspect that many can relate to my realization. How many times has something been intensified because we were fearful? Often, it is less about what actually happens to us and more about the fear of what could happen that stops our forward motion.

I've spent a lot of my life fearful and distrustful. I was afraid to fail and worried about succeeding. I was concerned about what people thought of me and terrified of humiliation.

WHEN YOU ARE AFRAID...

And dare I say that I was even scared of God. I spent my early childhood years raised in a denomination that taught me to fear God, because we never knew what He was going to do. Of course, I was that inquisitive child that kept asking "Why?"; however, I was told to "Never question God."

Yet, I'm not as quick to retreat into fear anymore because I have gone through experiences where God has taught me to trust Him, believe Him and believe **in** Him. And just like He protected me during that unforgettable horseback ride in the middle of the ocean, He will do the same for all of us in everyday life. The Word of God tells us, in Zechariah 2:8 NKJV, "...for he who touches you touches the apple of His eye." We are that special to our Father God. In fact, God tells us, in Isaiah 49:16 NKJV, "See, I have inscribed you on the palms of *My hands*; Your walls are continually before Me." This sounds like a very safe place to be. I'm not sure we can be more protected than within the palm of God's hands.

Nevertheless, there is a requirement on our part. We have to be courageous and step out of the boat. I believe that God wants the Believer to step out and **then** He meets us in that place of the unknown. He invites us on an adventure to trust Him, similar to when Peter stepped out of the boat to walk on the water (Matthew 14:28-29 ESV). I am sure you remember that He began to sink, but let's also not forget that Jesus was there to rescue Him. So, why would we fear this loving God?

This is what happened to my good friend Katie, who was unexpectedly diagnosed with a brain tumor. She loves to volunteer in her church and is a faithful Christian. Katie is just your average, good-natured person. She is the kind-hearted friend that most depend on for sound advice and seems to seldom, if ever, have a cross word to speak to anyone. In that critical circumstance that was completely out of her control, she decided to trust God. There were not any apparent reasons for the illness and the only cure was a risky surgery to remove the tumor. Katie underwent the required brain surgery, not knowing if she would live, die, or finish her years paralyzed, unable to speak or move parts of her body. It was an incredible challenge, but Katie eventually made a full recovery and returned to work, church, and enjoying a vibrant life with her family and friends.

Certainly, not every situation ends on a positive note. Real life is not like the movies. Sometimes people die, a relationship ends, and we never have clarity or answers. When we experience the unexplainable and don't understand, we must do the same as Katie did and choose to believe that nothing separates us from the love of God. It is our opportunity to judge God faithful.

If we are honest, many of us have lived in fear of God. Not the reverential fear that is really worship, but rather afraid of Him. Not realizing that He is our loving Father and cares deeply for us. When this first relationship is not in order, there exists a causal connection that causes all other relationships to be out of balance. So the overall question becomes: "Why are so many afraid?" I believe the answer is because we do not know Him.

I confess, it has taken many years to undue my wrong thinking about our loving God. Yes, God's ways are higher than our ways and there will be circumstances that are unimaginable and indecipherable, but we can be certain of the character of God. We discover His character by reading and meditating on the Word, which is our guide into how He thinks and acts concerning His children. Instead of assuming the worst, we should believe that God can be trusted. Sometimes, God has to demonstrate, through experience, His love for us in order for our limited thinking to comprehend the depth of His love. By

WHEN YOU ARE AFRAID...

demonstration, I mean going through some really tough predicaments and watching God prove His faithfulness.

When we are scared and unsure of how to navigate life's challenges, we can have faith that Jesus is with us, to lead us through the storms of life. As Jesus departed this earthly world, he told His disciples, in Matthew 28:20 NLT, "...And be sure of this, I am with you always, even to the end of the age." So when that next great opportunity comes your way, or life throws an unexpected curveball, take courage and step forward to meet it rather than shrinking back in fear, knowing that your trust is in a faithful, loving and powerful God. After all, God has not given us a spirit of fear.

PRAYER

Dear Heavenly Father, I pray that You would give my dear friends an extra measure of faith to believe and trust You, regardless of the circumstances. I pray that they would not retreat in fear, but rather move forward as You give them peace and favor. If they have failed in the past because of fear, I ask You to give them another chance to recover what was lost. In Jesus' Name, amen.

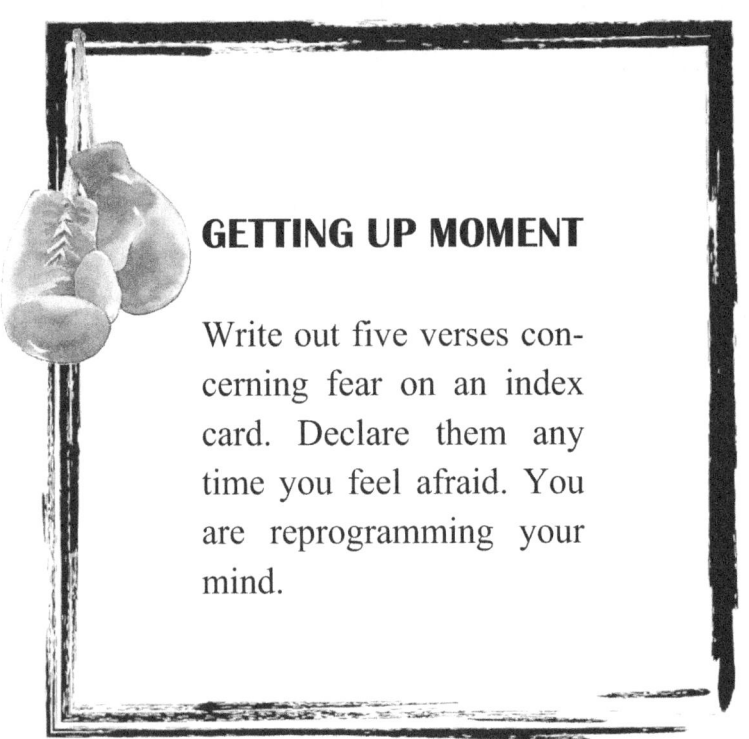

GETTING UP MOMENT

Write out five verses concerning fear on an index card. Declare them any time you feel afraid. You are reprogramming your mind.

-3-
WHEN YOU EXPERIENCE A HEALTH CRISIS...

"What do you mean there is nothing that I can do?" I sat in disbelief as my physician went on to explain that I would have to wait for my immune system to heal and get strong again. There was nothing else he could do. Just to be frank, I'm not necessarily known for being docile, but at that exact moment, a version of Cruella Deville was screaming on the inside. *Maybe she came out a little.* After all, I had many "important" things to take care of and apparently my health had not been on the top of that list. But alas, I had grown completely weary after spending month after month in the doctor's office for the same condition. The time had finally arrived where I was forced to prioritize my health. I am somewhat embarrassed to admit that it took a serious health scare to push me down the right road.

It seemed to me that the doctor needed to prescribe medicine and let me get on with my life, but that was not how this process was going to play out. Instead, I had to patiently wait, as my body gradually healed. There were various reasons why

GET BACK UP!

I found myself in that predicament, which pretty much all combined to me living under too much stress and not taking care of myself in the process. The list was sort of endless, but mostly comprised of missed meals and workouts, while surviving on caffeine and snacks. *I should probably own stock in a certain coffeehouse corporation.* Let me not forget to mention the effects of lack of sleep and isolation. So there I was, defeated and forced to slowly and methodically endure the process of getting well. I could no longer hide from the consequences of not caring for myself. I was the responsible party with no one else to blame. I allowed busyness and worries to have more value than my health. As I quietly contemplated, I apologized to God for not taking care of the body He had given me and purposed to do better. I always assumed that valuing health meant being skinny, but that's really only part of it. I started down the road of understanding. True health encompasses so much more than weight.

As I look back on that season, I can remember how difficult it was. It felt like walking through a dark valley as I was forced to slow down and rest, in order to get better. It reminds me of Psalm 23, which my grandfather loved and would often recite to me by memory. I can remember as a little girl that it was the scripture verse that he would often say before a family meal. As a young child, I didn't really understand the importance of the passage or its true meaning, except the part about goodness and mercy following you. I never asked Granddaddy why that particular Psalm was so special to him. Years later, I suspect it was the comfort of knowing that God is our Shephard and Protector. He is with us in the highs and the lows of life. Perhaps you agree that it is easy to see His hand of provision in the good times when everything is going well and we are having success. Yet, we are tempted to doubt His presence when things seem so hard and difficult. However, God is also

WHEN YOU EXPERIENCE A HEALTH CRISIS...

there during the low points, when life does not make sense and it seems like everything is falling apart. During those times, we are often believing in Him by faith, rather than seeing in real-time with our eyes.

During that season of suffering and pain, I felt helpless, ashamed, and alone. I didn't feel comfortable sharing my situation with many people because I thought surely everyone would think I must have done something wrong. After all, I was rather curvalicious. Secretly, I felt guilty. I asked God, *"What did I do to deserve this?"* My mind kept remembering all the bad things I thought about others. I think I repented for every sin I ever committed. I may have even repented for not taking the shopping cart back to the correct spot. Although I'm making light of this process, there are many who think if bad things happened to you, it means you have done something wrong. Sometimes that is the case, because life is about choices and there are consequences for sin and poor decisions. Yet, often painful experiences are just a part of life. They are unexplainable and not necessarily because of any "sinful" action. If there was a mistake made, then it was probably my decision not to have proper boundaries at work and take care of myself by making health a priority.

We also must acknowledge that there are times in life when we must press on and continue walking through a challenging season. It may not get better for a while. The road may be bumpy and rough until we reach our goal. We may fall down many times before it is over. Maybe you have been tempted to think that if you were God, you would do things totally different. But the truth is that God's ways are so much higher than our ways. Sometimes God leads us along that path that is rocky and steep. In those instances, He will strengthen us to climb and maneuver as stated in Psalm 18:32-33 NKJV, "It is God who arms me with strength, and makes my way perfect. He makes my feet like the feet of deer, and sets me on my high places." Regardless of the reason that we find ourselves in those difficult seasons, God is still with us. His rod and His staff comfort us (Psalm 23:4 NKJV). There are many situations that don't make sense to our natural minds. My challenge of being sick, month after month for over a year, was a deep valley for me. I could not enjoy a lot of activities that I would have normally participated in. For the most part, I was at home resting alone. As I would sit in the quiet, I was reminded of my grandfather's favorite Psalm. Psalm 23:1-3 NKJV is so very calming. "The Lord is my shepherd; I shall not want. He makes me to lie down in green pastures; He leads me beside the still waters. He restores my soul; He leads me in the paths of righteousness for His name's sake."

Ultimately, the seasons of suffering are really about trusting God. We are relying on His timing, provision, and protection. We come to know God's faithfulness as we experience His provision in difficult seasons in life. The lessons I learned about health and my immune system while walking through that lonely time has helped me for many years. I also have shared my lessons learned with so many other people to help them.

I still don't particularly understand why I went through that really tough, hard moment, but the experience has benefited me more than I can really express. I also learned that I can trust God to take care of every detail. The things that I was worried about passing me by during that season did not. In fact, either they waited on me, or they turned out not to be good for me anyway.

Since that time of sickness, I have had many more valleys to walk through and I suspect that more will come. I say this because it is impossible to live this life without difficulty. Anyone who tries to convince you otherwise is setting you up for

WHEN YOU EXPERIENCE A HEALTH CRISIS...

a major fall. Life is hard at times. Just like sheep, we get lost, we lose our way, or even experience opposition. With God as our Shephard, we can trust Him to pursue us, guide us, and protect us. In the midst of the pain and suffering of the moment, we must choose to declare that the Lord is our Shephard and we shall not want. This declaration of trust purifies our heart and brings us closer to the heart of the Father.

PRAYER

Dear Heavenly Father, I ask that You would comfort my dear friends as they walk through their personal valleys. I ask that You would heal their hearts and strengthen them as they walk the path You have for them. I pray that You would give them wisdom and insight to overcome every difficulty. May they overflow with Your joy and let it be their strength. In Jesus' Name, amen.

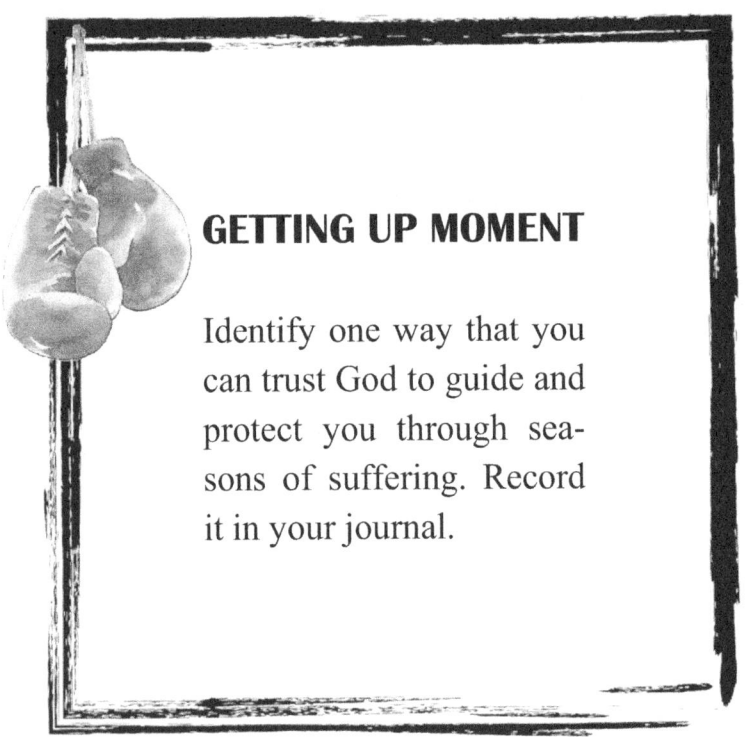

GETTING UP MOMENT

Identify one way that you can trust God to guide and protect you through seasons of suffering. Record it in your journal.

−4−
WHEN YOU NEED A NEW SELF-IMAGE...

There were two dresses clean in my closet that were appropriate for the morning's activities, but honestly only one fit—the burgundy, cold-shoulder, body-hitting dress. I stood staring into my closet, unable to comprehend how this happened to me. After all, I'm the girl who is super-organized and well planned. As I began my meltdown, I remembered the pile of laundry by the washing machine that I had promised myself I would finish and the other pile for the dry cleaners that I never found the time to drop off. What's the big deal, you may be thinking? Well, that form-fitting dress was clean and ready for a reason. I've only worn it once. Because I had no idea it would hit every curve in this curvy girl's silhouette when I bought it. I'm not sure what I was thinking when I initially purchased that dress. *Not entirely true, I wanted to be sexy.* However, the disapproving looks I got from others when I wore it caused me to put it in the back of my closet, never to see daylight in its future.

Yet, here we were, two years later, about to join forces again. I wish I could tell you that I jumped into that burgundy

GET BACK UP!

dress with enthusiasm and gusto, but actually I tried to squeeze into the other dress for about ten minutes. When I couldn't breathe or sit down for all my efforts to fit into my first choice, I then contemplated canceling my appearance. Although it was not a loud beaming voice from the heavens stating, *"You must wear the body con dress"*, alas it was a strong, quiet knowing that the day of reckoning had come for me to step out in it again. So I did. And discovered something unexpected.

It turns out I looked amazing! Yes, thick and curvy, but also beautiful and vivacious. I stared at myself in the mirror with disbelief. As recent Sunday School studies on insecurity flooded by mind, with reminders that we are our own worst critic, I decided to own my curves that morning. And I just pretended not to see any weird looks. This is where the story changes. Nothing happened in the same way that I remembered two years earlier. Instead of disapproving and critical looks, I received compliments and admiration. The only thing that changed from the first outing with that bomb-shell ensemble was the filter of my mind. I suspect the shift was in the attitude that I projected. When I decided to embrace every lump, bump, and bulge in that curve-enhancing dress, I believe I sent out a signal that I liked me and anyone who thought otherwise would have to defend a contrary opinion. This time around, I could see beyond my own negative self-image.

In the past, I had filtered all the reactions of others through my own negative self-talk. It's that inner critic (or voice in our heads) that judges, belittles, and tells us we are not good enough. When I wore my curvalicious dress before, I was so preoccupied and self-conscious about my body that I did not see my beauty. All I saw was a girl who has struggled her whole life with weight and never felt beautiful. It reminds me of the self-view of Gideon in the book of Judges, as he debated his ability to lead God's people to victory over the Midianites. In

WHEN YOU NEED A NEW SELF-IMAGE...

Judges 6:15 ESV, Gideon refuted how God saw him, "...Please, Lord, how can I save Israel? Behold, my clan is the weakest in Manasseh, and I am the least in my father's house." Yet, in Judges 6:12 ESV, God called Gideon a "mighty man of valor." Just as we see that the negative self-image of Gideon almost kept him from one of the greatest experiences of his time, my refusal to see my own beauty has hindered me in stepping out to embrace new opportunities and walking with confidence.

Just to be clear, I did not instantly overcome insecurity. It has been a process of moving forward with occasional steps back in the wrong direction. Gideon also had to grow into the champion that God destined him to become. As we continue reading in Judges, Chapter 6, we see that Gideon tested God several times to be sure God would give him victory. At a certain point and after much process, Gideon found his confidence and so will we. For me, it started with ignoring the negative thoughts that played in my mind. Instead, I chose to believe the affirmations I wrote on my bathroom mirror. At some point, after a very long period of back and forth, the destructive self-talk stopped.

This same type of thinking also affects our relationships with other people and (dare I say) our belief and approach to God. When we accept and like ourselves, regardless of our shortcomings and flaws, then we can accept and like others for who they are. Mark 12:31 NIV reads, "The second is this: 'Love your neighbor as yourself.' There is no commandment greater than these." Please imagine with me a world where we see the beauty and the value of people beyond pop culture, stereotypes and the projection of our personal self-image upon them. I believe this projecting on others is one of the causes of the cycle of harmful and destructive opinions that always circle back to ourselves.

GET BACK UP!

Dealing with insecurity and learning to accept ourselves is, unfortunately, common to so many women. One of the hardest things to do, at times, is to choose to like who we are just the way God made us—not perfect, but loved and intricately designed. In Ephesians 2:10 NLT, the Word of God states, "For we are God's masterpiece. He has created us anew in Christ Jesus, so we can do the good things he planned for us long ago." When I think of a masterpiece, I think of a priceless and extremely valuable work of art. Yet, I assure you, I was not confident as I prepared to walk out the door that morning. Instead, I had convinced myself that I was not good enough. Insecurity refers to a sense of self-doubt or deep feelings of uncertainty about our basic worth. Often there is a consistent negative dialogue in our thinking. There were voices and opinions, other than my own, that I amplified and allowed to have importance through the years. Yet, we cannot afford to allow the opinions of others (and the way they have treated us) to determine our value. In the end, it was my own thinking that held me back. What we think about ourselves matters so much more than what others think of us. Whether we are the little girl being made fun of on the playground or the grown woman giving her first presentation at work, the enemy uses deception to keep us distracted from seeing the truth of who we are. If God approves of us and accepts us, then why worry about what anyone else thinks? A wrong mindset believes that our worth is based on people rather than God. I believe that our worth is determined by the priceless sacrifice of Jesus (John 3:16-17 NLT).

WHEN YOU NEED A NEW SELF-IMAGE...

PRAYER

Dear Heavenly Father, I ask that you give my dear friends wisdom and a knowing that they are beautiful, accepted, and approved by You. Lord, I ask that You would restore to them all that has been lost—especially during all the times that they doubted Your truth, but instead listened and followed the negative self-talk in their minds. In Jesus' Name, amen.

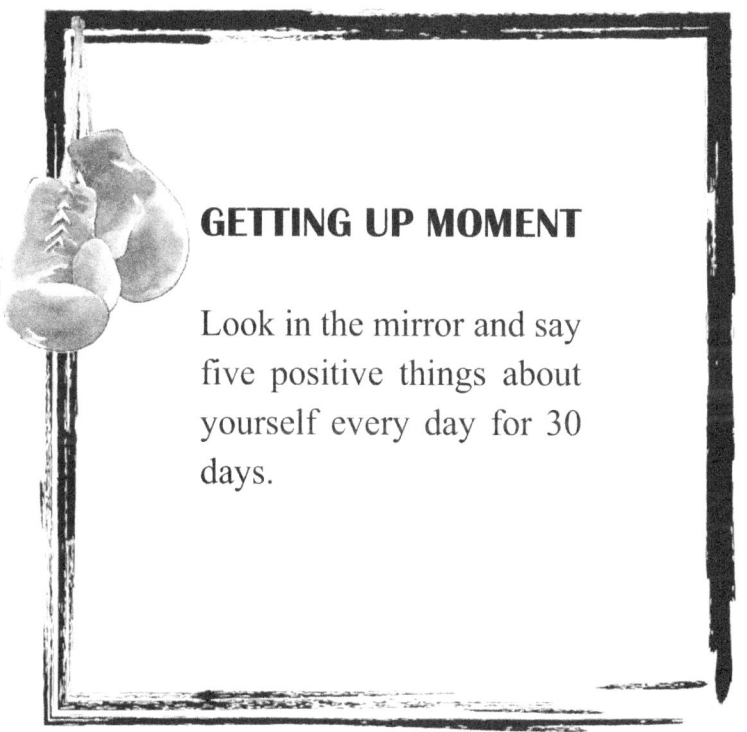

GETTING UP MOMENT

Look in the mirror and say five positive things about yourself every day for 30 days.

-5-
WHEN YOUR FAITH IS SHIPWRECKED...

In Acts 27, we find the Apostle, Paul, in the middle of a fierce storm and eventually shipwrecked on an island, after several intense nights at sea. It's probably safe to assume that the storm was not part of Paul's plan. The Scriptures indicate that his goal was to appear before Caesar to present his case regarding recent charges brought against him. Just like Paul, we may, at times, experience unexpected difficulty or opposition as we strive toward our goals and dreams. In fact, some of those circumstances can leave us feeling devastated and in shambles. In those trying moments, the question is often whether or not we will rise to meet the occasion with the heart of a champion or collapse in defeat on the sidelines with shipwrecked faith.

As I think of Paul's situation that stormy night, I recall a childhood experience that left me overwhelmed and unable to quickly bounce back. I finally summoned the courage to ride my bike without training wheels. *Oh joy, or so I thought!* This was a really big deal for me. Unlike most kids, it took me a very long time to learn how to navigate a bike and then even longer to ride

GET BACK UP!

with just two wheels. I'm not exactly certain of the reason for the delay. I'm told it had something to do with balance issues because I had braces on my legs as a toddler. Because of those mobility issues, my grandmother would watch me ride my bike from the oversized window in her living room (unbeknownst to me)—just in case I took a tumble. As it turns out, she was a very wise woman. Yes, indeed, I hit a hidden pothole and tumbled right off the bike and onto the road, which just happened to overflow with water from a creek gone out of its banks. There I was, sitting in the middle of the street, soaked and in tears.

You are probably thinking all I needed to do was stand, but for some reason I could not pick myself up. I felt helpless and humiliated. I forgot to mention that all the kids playing in the neighborhood playground saw my fall. *Did they have to see it? I'm already slower than most of them in learning to ride a bike.* As I sat there paralyzed by shame, I saw my uncle running towards me. You see, my grandmother saw me fall and immediately sent reinforcements to help. With a performance worthy of an Oscar, I, without hesitation, let my uncle carry me the whole way home.

The helplessness I experienced that beautiful, sunny day, while drenched with water, is the same emotion I felt twenty years later, as I lay face down on the carpet, wet from my own tears. I had come to the end of myself again, exhausted and unable to pick myself up. No longer able to live in denial, I had run out of options and finances.

I vaguely remember having the grand idea to go to law school. I had it all figured out. But just like Paul, the unexpected happened. My school was in some sort of trouble with the Department of Education and, long story short, there was a delay in releasing my student aid. If I did not get the money

WHEN YOUR FAITH IS SHIPWRECKED...

right away, I was going to be homeless. *Ok, homeless is probably a stretch.* I did have family in the area, but I was going to be extremely humiliated in the process of begging for food and a place to sleep. And as I lay prostrate on my floor, I heard the voice of the Lord say to me, *"Do you still not believe that I love you?"*

In other words, did I still doubt God would provide for me and come through when I needed Him? The truth is, I did not believe God would supply my needs in that moment. I thought if God were going to come through, He would have done so before then. Moreover, I deduced that I was better off trusting myself, rather than God. Where was the fearless girl with the child-like faith who was rescued in her moment of distress? What happened to the girl who had a dream and knew exactly where she was going? I used to be so courageous when I was young. Sometimes I look at my niece and I see glimpses of that former bravery. I had lost a part of that girl somewhere along the way. She forgot how to fight. She forgot how to believe. She forgot her faith.

After my own stormy night on land, I experienced the salvation of God with a miraculous intervention into my circumstances. God did, in fact, come through with the finances, but from another source unknown to me.

So, you may wonder how we avoid having our faith shipwrecked. In life, we will not always understand why we experience hardship and pain. Sometimes it is difficult to reconcile a loving God with struggle and loss. In those moments, when our faith does not quickly rise up to defend our heart, we can **trust** that an all-powerful and loving God will carry us.

Whether through a fall on a bicycle or any other failure, we have to rise from defeat. It is the getting up that makes us a champion. Not too long ago, I talked myself into a hiking trip in the Austin Hill Country that included the reward of a refreshing, natural

GET BACK UP!

swimming hole. I was not really in the best of shape for the trek on the rocky path. Plus, I had recently recovered from a car accident a few months prior. I did it anyway. I wanted to get out of my comfort zone and recapture my adventurous side. As I approached the final stretch of the steep incline, I needed to take a break. It was a hot, humid, exhausting day and a beast of an uphill climb. As I sat in the shade, I wondered if I could finish. I daydreamed of how nice it would be to have a helicopter to swoop in and transport me to the finish line, but that was not happening. I did think for a brief moment, *"What if I can't do this? What happens?"*

After a really good rest and some people checking on me from our group, I decided to get up and finish my course. As I rounded the last few steps, I heard a stranger near me say, "We are champions. We did it. We are bold. We are brave." Honestly, all I thought in that moment is, *"We are crazy for trying this!"*

Later I realized that the unknown person encouraging me was right. It takes the fortitude of a champion to persevere through the hard, difficult, moments in life to reach their dreams and overcome failures. We must have the attitude that we shall live to fight another day. I believe that the Apostle Paul must have had that same champion mindset, as he encouraged the ship's crew during the storm to keep moving forward.

Sometimes the broken places in our lives can try to sink us, but I believe, instead, God wants us to thrive. He wants us to rebound from the setbacks to believe again. Let's trust that God knows what He is doing and stay in peace, accepting that with Jesus in our boat, we will make it to the other side. Jesus will quiet our storms just as He rebuked the winds and calmed the sea for the disciples in Matthew 8:26 NLT, "Jesus responded, 'Why are you afraid? You have so little faith!' Then He got up and rebuked the wind and waves, and suddenly there was a great calm."

WHEN YOUR FAITH IS SHIPWRECKED...

PRAYER

Dear Heavenly Father, I ask that You give my dear friends the strength and fortitude to continue on and finish their race. Lord, You know the hardships and failures they have endured. I ask that You would restore their faith in You and joy for what is to come. In Jesus' Name, amen.

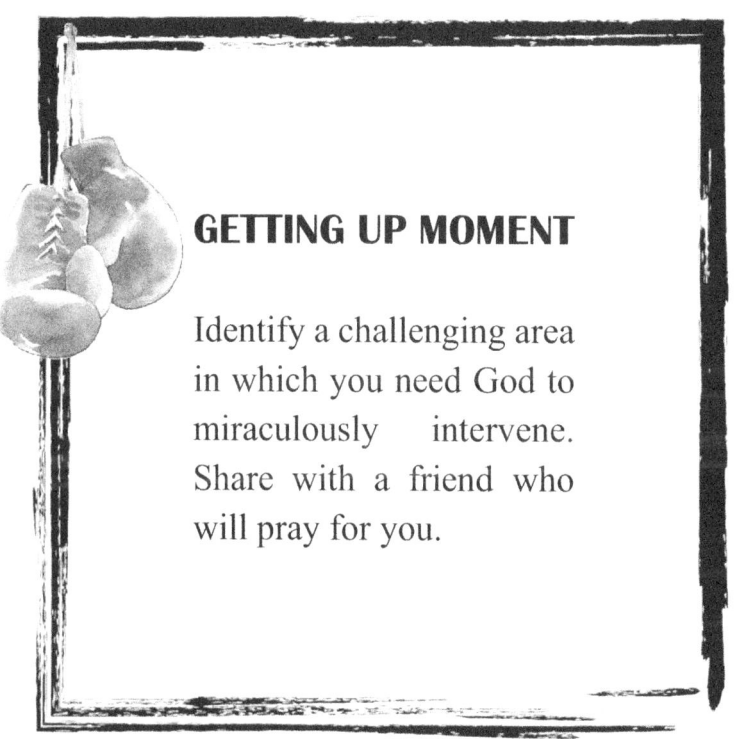

GETTING UP MOMENT

Identify a challenging area in which you need God to miraculously intervene. Share with a friend who will pray for you.

-6-
WHEN YOU FEEL LOST...

I could barely contain my excitement about attending a prestigious ladies luncheon at a very exclusive venue in Houston. Everything about this event soaked with prominence and prestige, from the well maintained grounds, to the doorman, to the properly placed table setting, and the string quartet. And then it happened. This immaculate, well accomplished mother of two, with a Ph.D. in Christian counseling sat next to me. The doctor asked two questions that changed my life, "So how is Nicole doing? What is inspiring her these days?"

Wonderful, I thought. Of all the women in this room for her to sit next to and analyze, God chose me. Perhaps you are thinking this is a simple question. Just answer it and quickly change the subject. At least that is what I told myself. The only problem—the answer was not simple, because I was not ok. I didn't feel inspired at that moment, nor had I for a long while. Life seemed dull and like a treadmill. With slightly misty eyes, I said "Great. I'm doing very well. Thank you for asking." I held in my emotions with every ab muscle I could gather.

I used to be excited about life. I had a dream and the passion to go after it. I was determined to reach my goals and fulfill my purpose, then something happened to my drive. It's like the wind was knocked out of my sail. Joy and hope were floating away. I didn't know how to get them back. I confess, this all snuck up on me when I wasn't looking. I was busy doing God's work—building His kingdom and making His Name famous. There were times that I was doing something church related probably every day, whether managing a singles coffee house, volunteering in the weekly church service, teaching Sunday school, or leading a professional women's group. I loved every moment of it.

Sometimes in life we know exactly where we are headed. The vision is so clear with an established and reliable route. Only, things change and disappointments happen on the way to achieving our dreams. It's kind of like an "old-school" road trip—before there were navigation systems. As a kid, my family loved to take summer vacations by car. My job was to navigate our way and read the map. You have to be prepared for the unplanned while traveling. There is always the possibility of construction, detours, accidents, bad weather, etc. The driver has to adjust to the road conditions unexpectedly without advanced warning. I can remember when we had to pull over and wait for the weather to clear in order to see the road. Life is the same way.

So, what do you do when you realize that you're lost and can't figure out the next step or the right turn? Well, you do the same as you would if you were on that road trip. You pull over, catch your breath, calm down, and look at your map. Only, our map is not a road atlas, but rather the Word of God. We are told in Psalm 119:105 NKJV that, "[His] word is a lamp to [our] feet and a light to [our] path." Likewise, we know from Psalm 27:11 NLT that God leads us along the right path for our life, which means that we can count on God to direct and guide us. Only, we have an action step—to seek His guidance. If you are

WHEN YOU FEEL LOST...

on that road trip, the absolute worst thing to do is to keep going in a direction that you are not sure is the right way.

There are always signs that you are on the wrong path such as exhaustion, lack of enthusiasm, no passion, and roadblocks. The things that once gave you such joy will be hard and difficult. You will find yourself complaining about the exact thing you prayed for so desperately to God. The temptation is to ignore these warning signs and explain them away. However, this place of denial is a trick of the enemy to lull you into complacency. If the enemy can't get you wrapped up in destructive patterns and bad habits to weigh you down, then his goal is to keep you from accomplishing the best plan for your life by dulling your passion.

As you re-evaluate and recalibrate your location, you may have to make a U-turn and go back to where you last had clarity. This is what happened to my friend Becky. She thought she wanted to go into politics. She ran for a political office, but she lost. Later, she found herself shunned by the winning political party and laid off by her employer. Becky thought she heard God clearly, but it did not work out. She had to take the time to find out her next step. Not too long after she began to seek God, she was impressed that it was time to start her own business. The interesting thing is that she had a law practice years ago, but it did not do well. When she dissolved her previous law office, it seemed the right thing to do because God was opening new doors. However, those same doors were closed to her. She could not see what God was doing in her life, but He had a plan that resulted in a thriving business.

There are quite a few ideas that I thought were great at their conception, but they were not God inspired. Later, I would ask myself, *"What was I thinking?"* It was all me charting my own course. When I look back, I know exactly how I got lost. I made a turn without relying on wisdom. I took that job that I really should not have taken. I let the busyness of life crowd out my time with God and reading the Word of God. I was so angry with God for the disappointments and setbacks that I stopped meeting Him in prayer. I would show up, but I would just sit there. Really, I walked away from God. I no longer trusted Him to take care of me. I only trusted myself. Just so we are clear, trusting myself has never gotten me anywhere worth writing home about. Seriously. But still, I thought I could trust myself more than God.

We get lost because we take our eyes off Jesus. We get so caught up in doing and performing, that we leave our first love. And months, years, perhaps a decade later, we look up and wonder how we got so off course. When we blame God and stop spending time with Him, we begin to drift. As Believers, we were not meant to live life so aimlessly. The distance widens in the same way as earthly relationships. Could it be the time to make your way back to God, even if you are angry? Although God does not cause the setbacks and disappointments, He does allow them. God has given us His wisdom to help us. In Proverbs, Chapter Eight, we are told that wisdom is calling out to us in the streets. Proverbs 8:2-3 NKJV states, "[Wisdom] takes her stand on the top of the high hill, beside the way, where the paths meet. She cries out by the gates, at the entry of the city, at the entrance of the doors:" We are to seek out wisdom so that we can stay on the right path for our lives.

So, my friend, I suspect you are wanting to know how to get your fire and passion back. Just like Dorothy in the movie, *The Wizard of Oz*, you already have what you need to make your way back home. Whereas Dorothy had those famous red slippers, Believers have a Heavenly Father Who is there, ready and waiting to rescue them and take them back to safety. Go back to your quiet time with God. Don't miss it. Return to Him and He will return to you (Zechariah 1:3 NKJV).

WHEN YOU FEEL LOST...

Research shows that agnostics believe in God, but see Him as a faraway deity that cannot be trusted to truly love and care for them. This is such a cunning strategy from the enemy, because it is the love of God that actually rescues us. When my passion was gone and I was at my lowest, it was the love of God that rushed in and said, "I love you." I didn't really believe it at first. I wondered how God could still love me after I had walked away from Him. But that is exactly what God does. He holds on to us even when we let go. The Word of God tells us that nothing can separate us from the love of Christ—nothing. It's the grace of God that rescues us. We sure don't deserve it. Many Believers think, deep down, that they may have earned this status, but there is nothing that we can do to earn our place. It's just a free gift that we will never deserve. If earthly parents know how to give good gifts to their children, then how much more will our Father in Heaven do the same for us (Matt 7:11 NLT).

Maybe you are thinking you can learn from this, so that you will never get lost again, but I'm not sure that is possible. Just like my family road trips every summer, the unexpected and unplanned seem to always happen in life. And when they occur, we have to react in the moment. Yes, I still believe that wisdom is there to guide us, but for a moment, or maybe a season, we may be lost as our course corrects and we get back to the right path. It's no different than taking a detour through new territory. And not only because we do not walk alone, but also because some of the most beautiful surprises and hideaways are discovered while traveling backroads and detours. We can trust the Lord to lead us and guide us no matter where we are.

PRAYER

Dear Heavenly Father, I pray for my sweet friends reading these words. Lord, although they may feel lost and without passion, You know their exact location. I pray that You would be close to them in this season and that they would feel Your very presence. Lord, do a turnaround in their lives. Show them the next steps to put them on the right paths. Restore to them the joy and passion inside Your purpose for them. In Jesus' Name, amen.

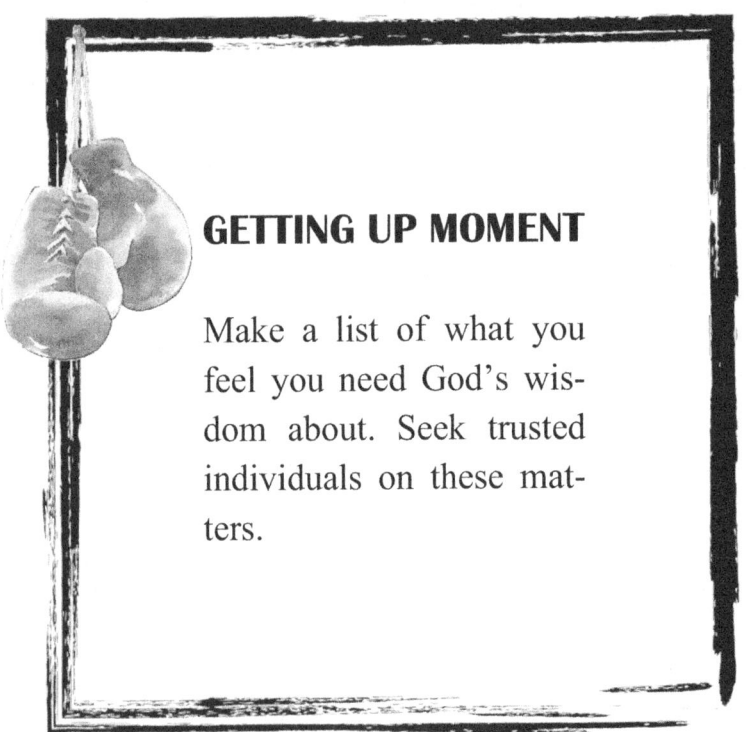

GETTING UP MOMENT

Make a list of what you feel you need God's wisdom about. Seek trusted individuals on these matters.

-7-
WHEN YOU ARE SINGLE LATE IN LIFE...

The annual trip home to Arkansas for Thanksgiving usually yielded the same question. "Are you ever going to marry?" Over time, I became quite skillful in responding with funny one-liners: "It's safely in God's hands. After all, He has the whole world in His hands." I still don't know the answer, but I sure hope so. I also must admit that I have a few questions for God regarding this subject. But as I wait, I choose to trust the Father's timing and provision. I have not always been confident in God's faithfulness in this area. For a long time, I believed a lie that someone spoke about me.

Instead of speaking life, a particular loved-one declared that something was wrong with me. He implied that my inadequacies were the reason that I was single. In other words, he might as well have said that I was not good enough to get married. I listened to the untruth and I allowed myself to believe it. What falsehood have you listened to about yourself?

It's really no different than the conniving scheme that satan spoke to Adam and Eve. After all, they were living the life of their dreams in the Garden of Eden. They had everything they could ever want. All Adam and Eve had to do was stay on the right path for their lives. But they could not do that because they were convinced that God was withholding something from them. We know, over six thousand years later, that our Heavenly Father was protecting them. But they did not know at the time that it was love and not punishment. In that moment, they chose their own way and pursued what they thought was best for themselves. When Adam and Eve mentioned their nakedness as the reason for hiding, God asked them in Genesis 3:11 NKJV, "…'Who told you that you were naked? Have you eaten from the tree of which I commanded you that you should not eat?' "

In the same light of earth's first couple's quandary, we must ask ourselves, "Who said we were "less than" for being single later in life?" Perhaps it was mom, granddaddy, our extended family, other Believers, or society in general. But, did God say it? Did He determine it was an unacceptable condition for us in this season? Probably not, and yet, we allow others to shame us in this way.

I suspect it is fear raising its ugly head in our lives. It's not easy to be different or to stand out. Going against the grain can be lonely and isolating at times. It forces others to look at themselves and challenge their decisions. The truth is that I know many people who did not marry for love. They married because all their friends were marrying or because he or she seemed "good enough" at the time. What if God was doing something new that would astound us if we could only push back the fear of being alone?

It took me a lot of years to undo that really bad thinking. I finally came to understand that there are any number of reasons why many find themselves single late in life. And still, we may never know the true reason for our delayed hope. What we can hold onto in the meantime, is that we serve a loving, faithful, kind, Father God. In this life on earth, there will be trouble, difficulty, and pain. Brokenness and hardship are not easy topics for the religious-minded. I suspect it is because it feels contradictory to reconcile a loving God with pain or grief. But part of trusting God, is understanding He is sovereign and there will be many things we don't understand. Instead, we look to His character.

For me, I have resigned myself that I'm just that girl—the girl who will marry later in life. I never imagined it would be me. Actually, I fought it and lived in denial quite a bit about it. I vaguely remember praying, "God, please do not let me be the last of my friends to get married." Yes, I already know what you are thinking. But, here I am; months, years, and many seasons of life have passed, and yet I'm still believing and waiting in my season of singleness.

Years ago, my pastors gave graduating seniors a framed scripture to guide them through life. For me, they chose Proverbs 3:5-6 NKJV, "Trust in the Lord with all your heart, and lean not on your own understanding; In all your ways acknowledge Him, and He shall direct your paths." I remember thinking, *"Great! What does this mean for me?"* I didn't know at the time that it was exactly want I needed. My trust in God has sustained me through these years. So many times we are busy looking at what we don't have, instead of seeing the beauty right before our eyes. Instead of spending time and energy begrudging your season of singleness, or really any season that is not the one you want, focus on the advantages of that season.

You see, love did find me. It just didn't look the way I thought it would look. Instead of that tall, dark, handsome, prince charming, it was accepting the unfailing love of my Heavenly Father. And this love affair has taken me on a journey that I never imagined in my wildest dreams—it's so beautiful and takes my breath away. And it has been my absolute pleasure to reap the fruit of wonderful friendships that I believe have changed my life forever. Plus, I've had the opportunity to travel the world and make lifetime memories. And contrary to what some singles believe, I do have permission to be happy. I have truly enjoyed my season of singleness. It is neither what I expected nor planned, but it has been fabulous. You, too, can enjoy your season of singleness.

Because of the Godly desire for a mate and our culture norms, many singles believe they will not be content and complete until they marry. These negative mindsets give singles the impression that they don't have permission to be happy. But God wants us to live a fulfilled life. To be single means to be separate, unique, and whole. Marriage will not satisfy an unhappy person. A healthy, fruitful life is available to every single person if they are submitted to God and serving Him with passion and purpose. Our love relationship with God is forever and not just until we marry. Paul said, in Philippians 1:6 MSG, "There has never been the slightest doubt in my mind that the God who started this great work in you would keep at it and bring it to a flourishing finish on the very day Christ Jesus appears." The season of singleness can be adventurous, exciting, full, joyous, and prosperous. It's all about our attitude.

For many of us, it's the hardest thing to be satisfied by who we are and what we have, instead of what we are not. Part of trusting God is having contentment, which brings true happiness and fulfillment. Take comfort from the words in Philippians 4:11-13 TPT, "I'm not telling you this because I'm in need, for I have learned to be satisfied in any circumstance. I know what it means to lack, and I know what it means to experience overwhelming abundance. For I'm trained in the secret of overcoming all things, whether in fullness or in hunger. And I find that

WHEN YOU ARE SINGLE LATE IN LIFE...

the strength of Christ's explosive power infuses me to conquer every difficulty." There are some seasons in life that are just special and to be remembered, almost like a gift that is especially wrapped for us. Perhaps, that is what the Apostle Paul, meant when he spoke about the gift of singleness (1 Corinthians 7:6-9 NKJV). The problem is that we never see singleness as gift, but more like a scarlet letter—shameful and hideous. Singleness is a gift, even if only for a season.

During your season of singleness, remember that God's grace is sufficient to sustain you. As stated in 2 Corinthians 12:9 NKJV, "And He said to me, 'My grace is sufficient for you, for My strength is made perfect in weakness.' Therefore most gladly I will rather boast in my infirmities, that the power of Christ may rest upon me." Your season of singleness is a great time to grow spirituality, develop yourself, discover your purpose in Christ, learn to manage your finances well, travel, and volunteer in the church. You can also focus on serving the Lord. Let's use this time to cultivate a deeper relationship with God and Christian friends (both single and married) to overcome loneliness. Singleness is a great season, in which to be open to new friendships. Loneliness is a lie from the enemy to discourage and steal your joy.

PRAYER

Dear Heavenly Father, I pray that you would strengthen and comfort my friends reading these words. Lord, give them peace and confidence that they can trust You with their desire for marriage. I ask that You give them a full community of friendships to support them during their season of singleness and fill their hearts with hope of the promise to come. In Jesus' Name, amen.

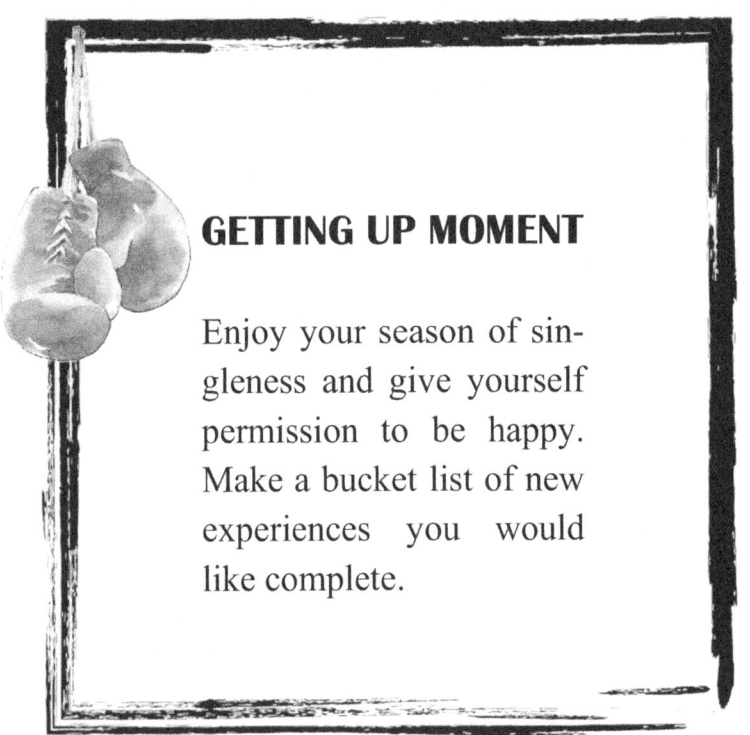

GETTING UP MOMENT

Enjoy your season of singleness and give yourself permission to be happy. Make a bucket list of new experiences you would like complete.

-8-
WHEN YOU FEEL FORGOTTEN...

A colleague mentioned that he was considering becoming a Christian. I knew him to be an agnostic and I had been praying for his salvation for quite some time. As he spoke that day, I began to reason and discuss with him why none of the other religions made sense for him, personally. Finally, I said, very emphatically, that his life would go better once he made the decision to follow Christ. Later that evening, I thought to myself that actually, his journey might get a little more painful and difficult. Although I completely believe things will improve over the long haul, it is highly likely that he will experience hardship and struggle as a Believer.

The life of a Believer is not easy. We live in a culture that seems to attack Christian values. Likewise, we have an enemy that is seeking to steal, kill, and destroy us. God has given Believers victory over every power that comes against them. However, the caveat is—it is the struggle and fight that makes us overcomers. Life as a Believer is not a walk in the park. Believers must fight with faith, grit, and the Word of God. There is no getting around it.

There are moments when everything seems to go our way

and we can see the results of our prayers. In those times, it is easy to anticipate that circumstances will be perfectly aligned with order and peace. Some refer to these seasons as mountaintop experiences because of the joy and emotional thrill of victory. During those conditions, it is easier to believe that we are more than conquers through Christ. Our confidence in God's love and provision is so certain after He shows up in a big way.

I distinctly remember such an experience. I had just accepted a dream job that pretty much doubled my salary and thrusted my career to the next level. I was beyond ecstatic. I prayed for that job and approached it like the walls of Jericho around my promised land. This was my mountaintop moment. I knew that God had given me the victory. However, I was not prepared for what came next. Six months after accepting that great opportunity, there was a restructuring in the company. All of a sudden, that victorious conquest became an almost insurmountable challenge. I no longer had the favor that I once enjoyed. Instead, I experienced persecution. At first, I doubled down on my prayers and confessions. My thought was that this was the enemy trying to steal my joy and promise. I was so certain that my God would come through quickly for me, as He had before.

There was only one problem. God did not rescue me right away. Instead, the days turned into weeks and the weeks turned into months. It would actually be eighteen long months before I was vindicated. It felt like God had forgotten about me. Life seemed like a fog and everything was blurry. The exuberance I felt on the mountaintop had evaporated into despair in the valley. All that was left were my petitions to God that were more analogous to a broken record.

The flawed thought is that the life of a Believer will be easy-breezy, with no troubles. I'm not completely certain where that thought began, but it is wrong thinking. Could the

WHEN YOU FEEL FORGOTTEN...

real problem be that our generation is weak and unconditioned for the hardness of life? In fact, numerous scriptures throughout the Word of God instruct Believers to be strong and courageous. In 2 Peter 1:5-6 NIV, we are told to add perseverance to our faith, "For this very reason, make every effort to add to your faith goodness; and to goodness, knowledge; and to knowledge, self-control; and to self-control, perseverance; and to perseverance, godliness;" In other words, we will need fortitude to journey through life, which encompasses strength, bravery, and resilience. When you think about the generations before us, they endured hardship with a sense of valor—from slavery, the Great Depression, the World Wars to the Civil Rights Movement. The struggle made them strong. Yet, most Westerners, today, have not struggled to that same degree. Some would even argue that most live as kings and queens, compared to other parts of the world.

Living the blessed, fortunate, privileged life that many have in America has a downside. We do not know true hardship and struggle. It's easy to stay committed to God when everything is going well. During those times, we almost feel like a favorite child. But what about those seasons when God does not come through when or how we expect Him? We are often not as confident of His love for us during those times. If we are honest, we probably think that perhaps God has forgotten about us. Actually, in reality, God is stretching us and asking us to trust Him. So much of getting back up, after you believe that God has overlooked you, is about trusting in His character, especially when life does not make sense.

I think about the life of Daniel. As a young Jewish boy, who was devoted to God, he, along with his countrymen, were taken captive into Babylon by King Nebuchadnezzar. This crisis extended for years. It would have been easy for him to feel abandoned by God and turn his back on his faith. Instead, Daniel remained faithful and full of spiritual integrity as he persevered through that difficulty. When Daniel was in the lion's den, he could have easily thought that God was not with him. Instead, he declared in Daniel 6:22 NKJV, "My God sent His angel and shut the lions' mouths, so that they have not hurt me, because I was found innocent before Him; and also, O king, I have done no wrong before you."

We are no different. There are some situations that frighten us and cause our thoughts to question where God is and if He will rescue us. In those instances, when it seems that God has failed us, that is exactly when we must trust in His faithfulness and loving kindness. But how often have you searched for Him with your five senses and could not find him? The silence often causes most Christians to doubt God's protection and whether or not He will come through for them. If this wrong mindset continues, then the fear of the unknown and the fear of humiliation manifests through negative thoughts as a defense mechanism.

As we wait, we are often sitting, or rather crouching, in the midst of pain and suffering. Most of us are confident that God is there because His Word says that He will never leave us or forsake us. No one tells you that a road of devotion will be hard when you give your life to Christ. I didn't mention it to my colleague, as he contemplated becoming a Christian. When we really stop and examine the life of the people in the Bible, we see a consistent thread of struggle and overcoming.

It is in those very trying situations that we must choose to believe that God is Who He says He is. There are some battles that have no alternate routes. Instead, we have to go through them in order to overcome. In the end, God is asking us to be strong and courageous as we trust in Him. Just as He reminded Joshua, in Joshua 1:9 NKJV, "Have I not commanded you? Be

WHEN YOU FEEL FORGOTTEN...

strong and of good courage; do not be afraid, nor be dismayed, for the Lord your God is with you wherever you go." We may not understand how things will turn out. I wish I could tell you that we will always get rescued, but I cannot. God's ways are higher than our ways and His thoughts are higher than our thoughts. I *can* tell you that we will always win when we stand in faith, even if that victory comes later into eternity.

Think about many of the heroes of the Bible in Hebrews, Chapter Eleven. Some of them perished, while standing in faith, yet not seeing the fruition of their prayers before they died. My own grandfather believed that God would answer his prayers for his grandchildren to be college educated and specifically for me to graduate from law school. Unfortunately, he passed away during my senior year of college. As a young adult, I often questioned how he could be so confident that God would help me to finish my studies. He believed, steadfastly, that God would fulfill his prayer request. Granddaddy had to trust in the faithfulness of God, even though earthly events did not work out for him to see it while alive. We cannot predict the end of our encounters, but we can trust the one Who controls the end and know with certainty that He is good, dependable and He loves us.

PRAYER

Dear Heavenly Father, I pray that You would strengthen my friends to walk through the hardships and struggles they face with persistent faith. May they have peace and fortitude to complete what You have set before them. In Jesus' Name, amen.

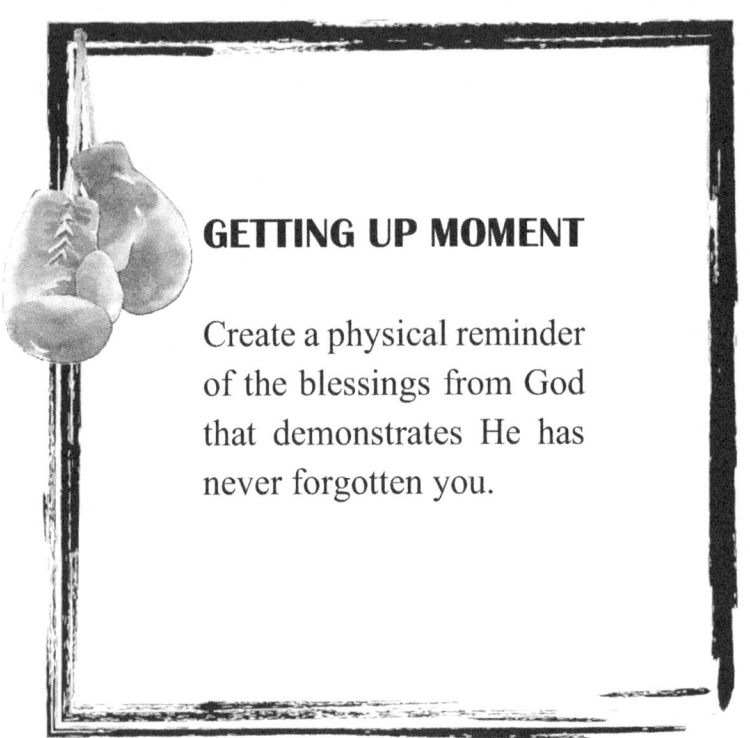

GETTING UP MOMENT

Create a physical reminder of the blessings from God that demonstrates He has never forgotten you.

-9-
WHEN IT'S TIME TO FIGHT...

My grandfather was a godly man and true patriarch of our family. He loved God, family, and people. My mom often reminisces that Granddaddy would say, "If you get into a fight at school, then you will be in trouble when you get home. But if you lose that fight, you will be in more trouble." *Granddaddy didn't play around.* His goal was not to encourage his children and grandchildren to get into squabbles, but rather to learn how to win and defend themselves. It would not occur to me until much later in life that often we must be taught both how to win **and** how to fail.

Unfortunately, Grandaddy had a lot more work to do with me. I was the little girl who would run and hide at the first sign of trouble. And our entire family knew it. Not to mention that I was always falling down or tripping and needing someone to rescue me. My cousins, on the other hand, were known for being tough and strong. I actually recall a grade school memory of feeling helpless when a classmate announced they were coming for me on the way home that afternoon at the bus stop. It's a vague recollection and probably something silly and childish, like stepping on someone's shoe or accidently taking their seat. Like I have said, I was clumsy and awkward in my younger years. All I remember is that when I got off that school bus, my tribe was there to back me up and walk me home. And just think. There were no cellphones to call for help at that time. I was covered. I didn't have to fight that day. However, unknown to me at the time, there would be many more battles to fight in the years to come.

As we grow and mature, the conflicts and difficulties are less about physical altercations, or a childhood tussle, and more about enduring and persevering in life. However, I believe we learn so much about our response to difficulty and setbacks in our formative years. Although I'm not that same timid child anymore, I must admit that I usually have to psych myself up for a skirmish. I'm not referring to physical squabbles, but rather spiritual battles.

We cannot predict or always prepare for every challenging circumstance we will encounter in life. What we can know for certain is that we will encounter these faith challenges along our journey. Believers are told in 1 Peter 5:8 NKJV, "Be sober, be vigilant; because your adversary the devil walks about like a roaring lion, seeking whom he may devour." This means that challenges, hardships, and trouble will come across our path at some point in life. Yet, we **do** have choices. We can try to avoid the conflict, like a turtle with its head in a shell. We also can give up by running away or we can stand our ground and fight the good fight of faith. The option to run and hide is not really viable because we have an enemy whose sole purpose is seeking to "kill, steal, and destroy" Believers.

If you are like me, you may try to compromise or even become overly accommodating just to avoid the conflict. Yet, there are times when it is unavoidable. I assure you that I have prayed (and quite possibly begged) God to shield me from experiencing hardship. However, many times God was silent or

WHEN IT'S TIME TO FIGHT...

wanted me to stay the course. Instead, I learned sometimes the victory is knowing that God is with you in the storm, walking with you through every challenging moment. And just like my encounter with the bully on my school bus, I have come to the realization that we cannot always avoid a fight. The good news is that, as Christians, we prepare for the battle and show up, but the victory belongs to God. He is there to back us up.

One of my favorite film trilogies is *Lord of the Rings*. In the movies, a group of individuals referred to as "The Fellowship" must undertake a journey to destroy an evil power ring. This quest becomes their life mission and binds the group together as friends. As they move forward to complete their assignment, there are many conflicts, setbacks, and unexpected complications they must overcome. There are many moments when it seemed they would fail and other times that sheer grit pushed them on to the next phase. We also have a purpose. The Word of God states, in Jeremiah 29:11 NIV, "For I know the plans I have for you," declares the Lord, "plans to prosper you and not to harm you, plans to give you hope and a future." The journey will include unplanned challenges, detours, or dead-ends that we must endure in order to complete our destiny. Similar to The Fellowship, there are people in our circle who will come alongside us as we accomplish our expected end. Their support and assistance will often make the difference in furtherance toward our target.

The Apostle Paul teaches in Ephesians, Chapter Six, that we must equip ourselves to stand against the schemes of our enemy. In verse thirteen, NIV, he states, "Therefore put on the full armor of God, so that when the day of evil comes, you may be able to stand your ground, and after you have done everything, to stand." If we want to keep the many blessings that God has given us and also move forward to accomplish all that we are supposed to, then we must learn to stand our ground. We have to decide that we are not giving up, but rather fighting through with prayer and our other spiritual weapons, no matter what our emotional state. We can endure the difficulties and challenges of life and fight for our dreams and goals as we are strengthened through Jesus. We can't be wimpy, whining Christians if we want to see victory and experience success in our lives. Ultimately, it's about faith and trust in God. It's about believing that God will come through for us and fight for us (be our refuge in times of trouble). In the end, all we have to do is show up for the battle, because the victory belongs to God. If we want to see the promises of God come to pass in our lives, we will have to learn how to fight for them.

WHEN IT'S TIME TO FIGHT...
PRAYER

Dear Heavenly Father, I pray that You will strengthen my dear friends for the road ahead of them. Lord, give them courage, boldness, and confidence that You are with them and will be with them in trouble. I ask that You make their justice shine like the noonday sun, as Your Word says in Psalm 37:6. Thank You Father that You are a shield of protection surrounding them. In Jesus' Name, amen.

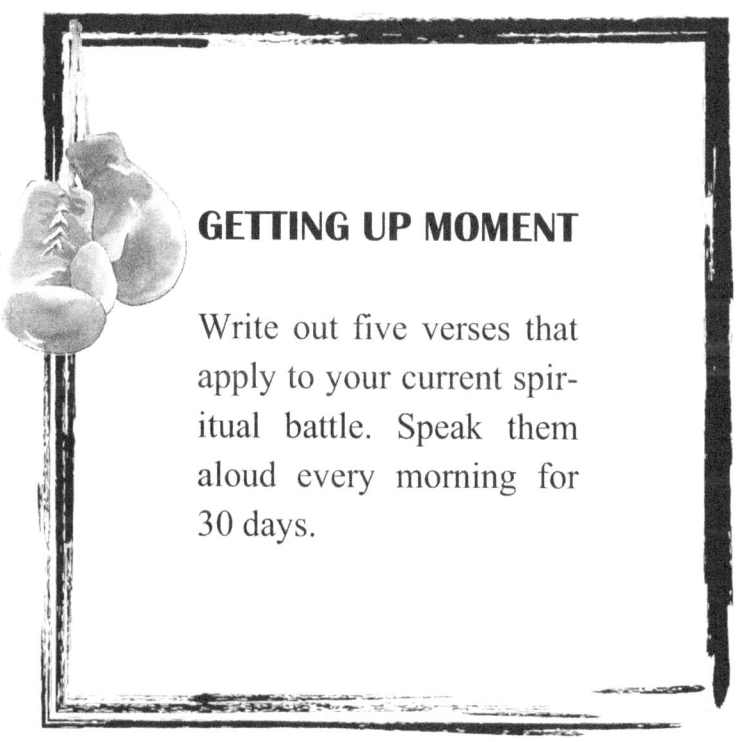

GETTING UP MOMENT

Write out five verses that apply to your current spiritual battle. Speak them aloud every morning for 30 days.

-10-
WHEN IT'S TIME FOR A CHANGE...

A good friend purchased an executive coaching package for me as a Christmas gift. *Great! Why could she not have just given me an ugly sweater that I could exchange later?* Now, this super private girl (meaning me) has to go reveal her innermost thoughts to a stranger. I have never before asked the advice of a life or executive coach. There was just never a need. That's probably a lie and a prideful one. I just never felt compelled enough to go. Plus, I have several friends certified in this area and they usually feel free to give me their opinion of my life all the time. I tried my best to avoid the coach. I was thinking of not claiming the gift, but she kept reaching out to me. So with really no options to escape, I scheduled the meeting, thinking I would go through the motions. In preparation for the first session, I was required to complete a self-assessment test.

It was there in the middle of finishing the pre-work that I finally understood the anger, frustration, and overall discontentment I had been feeling for a while, but could never articulate. My answers to the executive coach's tool revealed the problem—I was ready for a change. My current interests and passions no longer matched my present occupation or my education. It feels sort of like preparing your whole life for one path, but shifting to move forward in a completely different way. What are you supposed to do when you want change, but are not sure you are ready to face the consequences that come with that decision?

As I completed the homework from the executive coach, I realized that I was frustrated because I could not identify what changes were necessary. I just knew something was not right. I suspect my discontentment was showing up everywhere. I could sense it with a lost passion, dulled enthusiasm, and overall irritability. It was not easily detectable by others because I'm usually bubbling over with joy. But I guess my dear friend could also see it. I asked her why she purchased the sessions for me, and she said, "You need some help to get your life together." Despite the sticker shock of her words, I knew in my heart that she was right.

From that self-assessment and first session with the coach, I learned more about myself in 24 hours than I had ever known before. Turns out, there is this creative, enterprising, and entrepreneurial girl screaming on the inside. She wants out, to have fun and be free. Keeping her contained and forcing her to live at a low level was hindering and it was starting to affect other areas of her life. I'm told that I was operating in two lanes: one as a lawyer and one as a writer/creative type. Everything seemed fine, until it was no longer fine. I felt fulfilled, passionate, and purposeful operating in both worlds and I just assumed this would be my life. Apparently, many people can operate in multiple lanes for a long time until they reach the point where they are exhausted. They don't want to juggle life anymore.

In no way am I suggesting that we should forge ahead because we no longer feel excitement about our life. Instead, I present to you that it is possible that God wants to shift us into

WHEN IT'S TIME FOR A CHANGE...

our purpose with His wisdom and direction at the right time. Sometimes, God will surprise us with new dreams that are different and often bigger than we could imagine on our own. This is what happened to me. I started a faith-based professional women's group at my church with a few friends. At first, it was just a hobby to network and connect with like-minded, young, Christian professional women. But nineteen years later and after the "young professional" part has passed, it has become a passion and purpose-filled. I was surprised by God. I did not see it coming. I did not expect it to bring me such joy and fulfillment. And so I began to maneuver through two parallel roles of business lawyer by day and creative/enterprising ministry leader by night. However, my test results showed what I could only sense—I was growing less and less attached to my profession. And, it was beginning to exhaust me.

When we experience these "divine intersections," I believe that God is putting, into our hearts, a desire to answer the call to purpose and the passion for exploration of the adventures we are meant to have with Him. Although it is a hidden desire that we are probably not able to articulate, it is then that we must search for it. The Word of God states in Jeremiah 33:3 ESV, "Call to me and I will answer you, and will tell you great and hidden things that you have not known."

Ultimately, any discontentment we feel is an absence of clear understanding of God's direction for our life. It's so easy, in the hustle and bustle of life's responsibilities and commitments, to be busy and overlook seeking guidance from God. When we spend quiet time with Him reflecting on His Word, our fears and anxiety are hushed, and we can hear His direction. We were not designed to carry these burdens and worries by ourselves.

There are other times when we know God wants us to take the next step toward our purpose, but we are scared. When the

GET BACK UP!

coach challenged me to pursue my passion full time, I immediately thought about my finances and the sacrifice undertaken to reach success in my career. I wasn't ready to give up on years of hard work. I questioned if I could make enough money to live at the level I had become accustomed to. I wasn't really ready to walk away. It was beginning to become uncomfortable walking on two paths, but not enough to stop.

So, I decided to stick it out a little longer and continued on. I'm not sure if I was expecting to magically shift back to life before I met the executive coach, or I was just avoiding the situation. A year later, I was in the same place. Stuck. Unable to move forward. And paralyzed by fear. I often think about the disciples when they answered the call to follow Jesus. They left their vocations and livelihood with no certainty for their futures. Answering the call of purpose will often require trust in God and faith in Him to provide for us. The disciples set off into unchartered territory without a map and not knowing how the end would turn out.

What do you do when it's time for a change, but you lack the courage? You take a step, even if it's a tiny one. I'm not entirely sure who convinced us that we have to quit suddenly and turn 180 degrees. It is possible to make gradual changes that move us forward. The wildest thing happened as I started toward my desired goal. My attitude improved, my passion came back, and my energy increased. I no longer felt like a victim who was trapped doing what other people expected of me. I found my voice. Although its volume was low and squeaky at first, it is slowly getting stronger; and I believe I will roar soon.

Change is not easy. Especially if we have been stuck in the same routine and people are only familiar with us in that way. However, remaining in a place of unfulfillment is also not wise, particularly when we sense our passion and purpose is for something else. If we don't address the issue, it will begin to

WHEN IT'S TIME FOR A CHANGE...

affect other areas of our life. As a Believer, we do not journey alone haphazardly regarding these matters. For truly God is with us as stated in Psalms 16:11 ESV, "You make known to me the path of life; in your presence there is fullness of joy; at your right hand are pleasures forevermore."

PRAYER

Dear Heavenly Father, thank You for being with my dear friends and keeping them along the right path for their lives. I ask You to fill them with joy and wisdom as they move forward in the purpose You have for them. Lord, give them direction to know which opportunities are right for them and the patience to wait on You and Your perfect timing. Lord, show them ways that they can move forward without getting ahead of You. In Jesus' Name, amen.

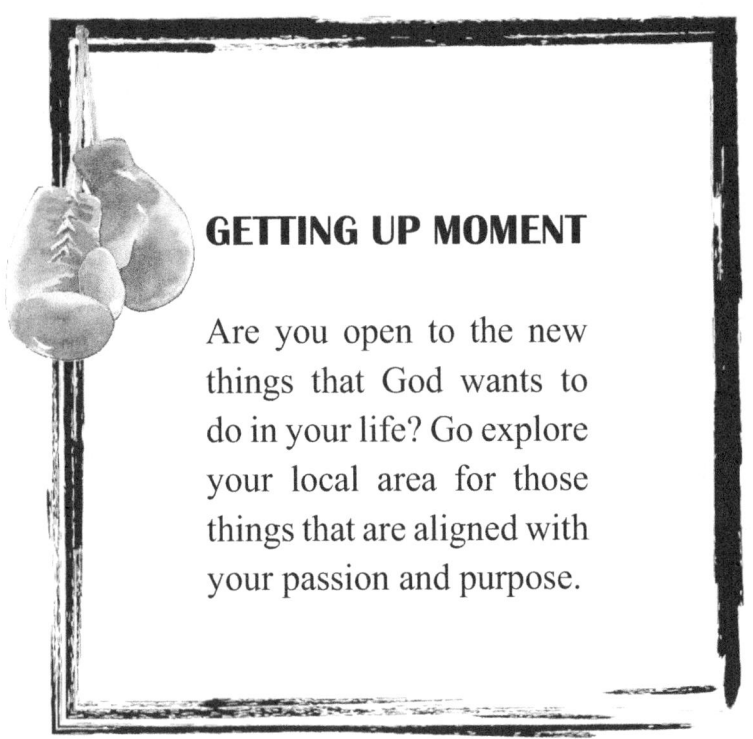

GETTING UP MOMENT

Are you open to the new things that God wants to do in your life? Go explore your local area for those things that are aligned with your passion and purpose.

-11-
WHEN YOU TAKE STEPS OF FAITH...

I can probably count on one hand the times that I have been truly surprised in my life. As I sat and listened to my boss explain how I did not meet expectations, I could feel my insides begin to twist and turn as worry, anger and anxiety mounted all at the same time. *How could this be?* After all, I truly believed that I served my boss and that job with integrity, joy, and excellence. I felt I brought my best self to work every day. But as I sat there quietly trying to hold it all together, an unwavering peace flooded me. I knew instantly what the lesson was for me. You see, not too long before then, I had a new opportunity come across my path. Most people would have leapt at it. But, instead, I rationalized why it was not a good fit for me. I actually remember saying that my boss would cry without me, because he loved me so much. I could see how I would disappoint him by leaving. The truth is that I was guilty of looking on the outside, instead of with my spiritual instincts. I was persuaded by so many former colleagues who told me, over and over again, how they could tell that my boss valued me. I secretly found security in their words and reassurances. It was almost as if I was willing to disappoint God for the supposedly sure thing that I could see. Don't judge me here. In the end, we are all made of dirt. I was consumed with the accolades of Man's approval over God's direction.

So, I decided that the new opportunity could not carry me where I ultimately wanted to go in life and thus was not for me. But I was wrong. So very wrong. I was so busy looking at everything in the natural that I missed what God was doing for the future. Looking back, I truly believe in my heart that God was opening a way of escape for me. He knew that hardship and persecution was coming. He was trying to direct my steps around it.

Sure enough, several months later my boss did a complete reversal from what I had previously seen and experienced working with him. Gradually, I no longer had the favor of doing no wrong. I now know in my heart that the lesson God was allowing me to learn is that we have to always look with our eyes of faith, rather than what we see in the natural. We have to follow His direction, even when we don't understand and it does not make sense to us.

Stepping out in faith means that there will be times when we take risks and open ourselves to failure. Trusting God, as we journey through life, means that each step is not always going to make sense. In the movie, *Raiders of the Lost Ark*, Indiana Jones, the hero of the movie, reaches a point in his quest where he must walk across a bridge to the other side of this massive cave over a seemingly bottomless pit. The only problem is that there was no bridge in sight. He finally decided to kick dirt into the air to see any kind of path—and part of a bridge showed up. He then decided to take another step into what looked like thin air, trusting that the bridge would be there. At each step, the bridge appeared, until he finally made

WHEN YOU TAKE STEPS OF FAITH...

it across the expanse.

Just like the character, Indiana Jones, we must take steps of faith into what sometimes appears to be the unknown. It is very easy to adapt to a safe and comfortable lifestyle and follow the path of least resistance by avoiding challenges. However, an essential element of faith in Christ is the willingness to take risks. Taking risks are hard sometimes because they open us up to the possibility of failure, which can be a little scary and intimidating, if we are honest. However, we are also opened to the possibility of reaching our goals or even an accomplishment beyond our wildest dreams. For many of us, it is uncomfortable learning something new, but the opposite is stagnation. There is a common saying in the corporate world that if you are not moving forward, then you are falling behind. Certainly, taking risk just for a thrill, is not wise. It is actually rather reckless. But, playing it safe is also unwise. They are both emotional responses, instead of faith-filled steps.

When I think about the new opportunity that I was presented with, I focused on all the possible negative consequences and what could go wrong. It did not occur to me that God was trying to bring something amazing into my life and also provide a safer, calmer, detour to my journey. I think that sometimes life is this way for many of us. The path may not be clear. It may not look like it is the right way, but we have to trust that God is directing our steps. It is then that we are able to surrender to peace.

When the children of Israel were about to embark on a new opportunity in the Book of Numbers, Chapter Thirteen, we find them on the threshold of the Promised Land and faced with a critical choice. They can opt for the path of least resistance or they can dare to trust God. Eventually, they scouted out the land, sized it all up, saw the giants, contemplated the difficulty and got scared. The Word of God states in Numbers 13:33 **KJV**

GET BACK UP!

"And there we saw the giants, the sons of Anak, which come of the giants: and we were in our own sight as grasshoppers, and so we were in their sight." We are no different. When an opportunity is presented to us, we also have a choice. We can either step out into the unknown or shrink back in fear.

I'm not sure if that opportunity, or even one similar, will ever come back around. I have to believe in my heart that it will. I believe that God has mercy on us and gives us a second chance. For the children of Israel, that next opportunity came through their descendants when God commanded Joshua to get ready to cross the Jordan River into the Promised Land. The Word of God states, in Joshua 3:8 NIV, "Tell the priests who carry the ark of the covenant: 'When you reach the edge of the Jordan's waters, go and stand in the river.' " There are many historians who believe the water reached hip level on the priests before it became dry ground. Our takeaway is that there may be times when we have to take a faith step toward our dream, even when it doesn't look like it will turn out right, that the outcome is not clearly in our favor, or it is uncomfortable.

Maybe it's time for you to take a step of faith. Sometimes risk taking is just about moving incrementally toward the goal, like Indiana Jones. There are so many successful businesses that start while the owner is working a full-time job, or books that are written as a side hustle. The risk sometimes becomes overwhelming when we try to know or anticipate every step along the way, but if we focus on just the next, best, singular thing it is manageable.

Finally, in order to seize new opportunities and take new ground, we have to get used to feeling uncomfortable and come to terms with the fear of failure and the fear of the unknown. We must quote Hebrews 13:6 NKJV to ourselves, "…The Lord is my helper; I will not fear. What can man do to me?"

Sometimes fear can be a warning that danger is up ahead.

WHEN YOU TAKE STEPS OF FAITH...

Other times, fear is a lie from the enemy trying to hold us back. In order to tell the difference between cautiousness that is warranted and fearful emotions deceiving me, I use the following guidelines: Is the opportunity in my heart and do I have a passion for it? Have I prayed about it? And have I sought out Godly counsel? There is a difference between lack of peace and fear. Fear will have anxiety attached to it.

After repenting and forgiving myself, I made a decision to step out next time and trust God, even if it doesn't make sense to me. I wish I could tell you that my epiphany caused everything to fall back in alignment, but it was not that easy. I actually had to journey through a very difficult season in my career. It was not wandering in a wilderness for forty years, but it was sufficiently grueling enough for me to learn not to hesitate when God is moving. Life is just better when we take the step of faith with our loving Father, rather than the false comfort of the fickle approval of Man.

PRAYER

Dear Heavenly Father, I ask that You would give my dear friends an extra measure of faith to move forward with You, especially when the circumstances around them do not measure up to their expectations. May they have the courage to believe You over what they see with their natural eyes. May they always seek to obey You over pleasing Man. In Jesus' Name, amen.

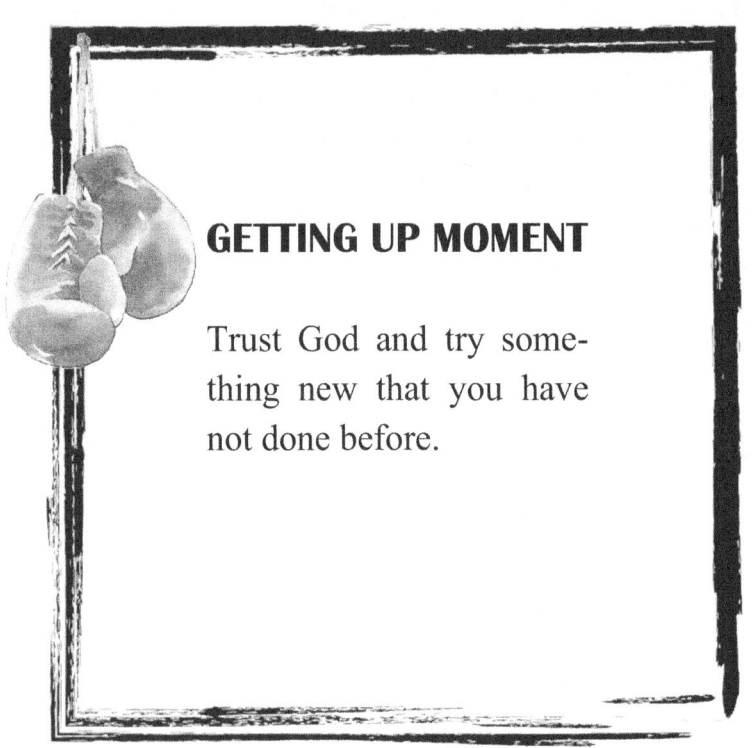

GETTING UP MOMENT

Trust God and try something new that you have not done before.

-12-
WHEN YOU ARE TEMPTED TO HATE...

For as long as I can remember, I have loved to read. I would stay up way past my bedtime, just so that I could finish a book. I always regretted it the next morning, as I struggled to stay awake. I can even recall reading with a flashlight under my bed covers, as a youngster. So, it should be no surprise that I eventually started a book club as an adult. In fact, this group of women, in my monthly book club, became some of my closest friends. Often our discussions form rabbit trails that travel deep into personal matters that preoccupy us at any given time.

Such was the case one particular evening, as we were discussing injustice. I don't really remember what book started us on our journey. However, before the end of the night, there were several unique experiences shared that expressed similar feelings of being wronged and violated. I recall one book club bestie describing the hatred and anger rising inside of her whenever she interacted with her foe. It felt so unfair to her. She believed nobody cared. She continually tried to rationalize how a loving God could allow such detriment to go on.

As I warmed my hands by cupping them around my mug of hazelnut latte, I contemplated my own feelings of injustice. And there were times when it seemed that God forgot about me, especially at work. Although the persecution I felt at the office did not involve a physical injury, wrongful convictions, or abuse, it was still quite painful to interact with people who, I felt, I had been wronged by and who benefited from suspect actions. I, too, had to interact with people who caused me to feel offense and unforgiveness rising in my heart. I prayed constantly and regularly petitioned God to intervene for over a year, but He remained silent. Like my sister-friends in the book club, I sometimes questioned if the Lord cared about my predicament and my pain.

As Believers, we don't often talk about loving God and dealing with offense and hatred at the same time. I suspect that is because it's not good Christian behavior. But also, because we can't sort out how we can love God and hate our neighbor. After all, loving our neighbor is a cornerstone of the Christian faith. And hate is such a strong word. It means an intense or passionate dislike for someone. I knew that I had to guard my heart from allowing the enemy to sow seeds of hostility within me. I can remember crying out to God to help me forgive and help me to love those that I found unlovely. I truly did not understand why I was going through that difficult moment. It seemed like I was all alone in my frustrations.

I learned a valuable lesson in that season that I know will help me for years to come. I shared it with the ladies that night in our discussion. I am convinced that sometimes it's just about overcoming the temptation to hate. I truly believe that if we can forgive, then we will pass the test. For the record, I know I've flunked a couple times. Just being real. I was given more chances to retake the test and succeeded. I had to learn the im-

WHEN YOU ARE TEMPTED TO HATE...

portance of surrendering, which opened the doors to forgiveness and freed God to do fantastic things in my life. Surrendering removes the traces of bitterness and allows us to breathe in joy and the new thing that is trying to form in our lives.

There are going to be times when there is such a personal attack that it is hard to let it go. These experiences can cause you to lose your perspective, even if for just a little while. I am referring to those situations that are a complete lack of respect of the value we bring as human beings. In those times, you should take the actions necessary to protect yourself—mentally, physically, and emotionally. We can surrender to the Lord and forgive offense, while still removing ourselves from a toxic environment.

I previously thought of surrender as giving up and quitting. I now realize that sometimes walking away from a fight or turning the other cheek is actually the way of love, humility, and ultimate healing. In that action, we are surrendering our right to defend ourselves or seek retribution and, instead, trusting our Heavenly Father for His justice.

The same mercy that we ask God to give us is also given to the person who seems so undeserving to us. With those thoughts, we have unknowingly elevated ourselves to the position of determining if they are worthy of mercy. We don't get that power. Stepping into the role of judge and jury, to determine who should receive His love and forgiveness, in our view, is one of the root causes of hatred in our hearts.

I found in my own life, when I am tempted to hate, it usually means that I have stepped out of hope and faith and into fear. When we take our eyes off of God and focus on the problem, then we really are making that problem bigger than Him and arguably creating an idol.

The truth is that God could easily turn that unfair situation around in a moment's notice, but He often doesn't. Instead, He allows us to exercise and strengthen our faith as we wait on Him to deliver us. I also submit to you that He is wanting to produce patience and trust in our lives. As the Word of God states in James 1:2-3 NKJV, "My brethren, count it all joy when you fall into various trials, knowing that the testing of your faith produces patience. But let patience have its perfect work, that you may be perfect and complete, lacking nothing."

Patience is not something we often actively seek out. Instead, faith is usually the primary pursuit. Of course that makes sense considering the Bible tells us that it is impossible to please God without it (Hebrews 11:6 NKJV). However, if we focus only on faith, we will give up when it is hard and before we triumph over our difficulties. As we endure, we are also learning to have patience through tough situations until they are resolved. Growing in patience as you wait on the Lord helps you to attain the promises of God.

In the middle of hard experiences, we have to wait on and trust the Father. We are trusting in His character, faithfulness, lovingkindness, mercy, and justice. How comforting to know that we serve a God of justice. We should be patient with others as they fail us and make mistakes. Likewise, we are to be patient with ourselves as we grow into the person God is shaping and maturing us to be.

Another aspect of overcoming the temptation of hate is not allowing that person or circumstance to steal our joy or cause us to fail to celebrate the good things in our lives. Although I experienced a lot of persecution during that trying period in my life, I also had a lot of success and great delight. We cannot allow our lives to be defined by a person or an experience. Instead, we must trust that God knows exactly what He is doing. His timing is perfect. I do not imagine that we will jump up and

WHEN YOU ARE TEMPTED TO HATE...

down about how the offensive actions were good for us. However, years later, we will know that we are handling a new matter better because of those previous experiences.

PRAYER

Dear Heavenly Father, I pray that You would give my dear friends the strength and grace to forgive those who have wronged them. Although they may not understand why it happened, I ask that You give them peace. Remind them that You are with them and will protect them as they walk through it. Father, every time they are tempted to worry or anger is rising in their hearts, encourage them that You are the God of justice. May Your joy overflow into their lives. In Jesus' Name, amen.

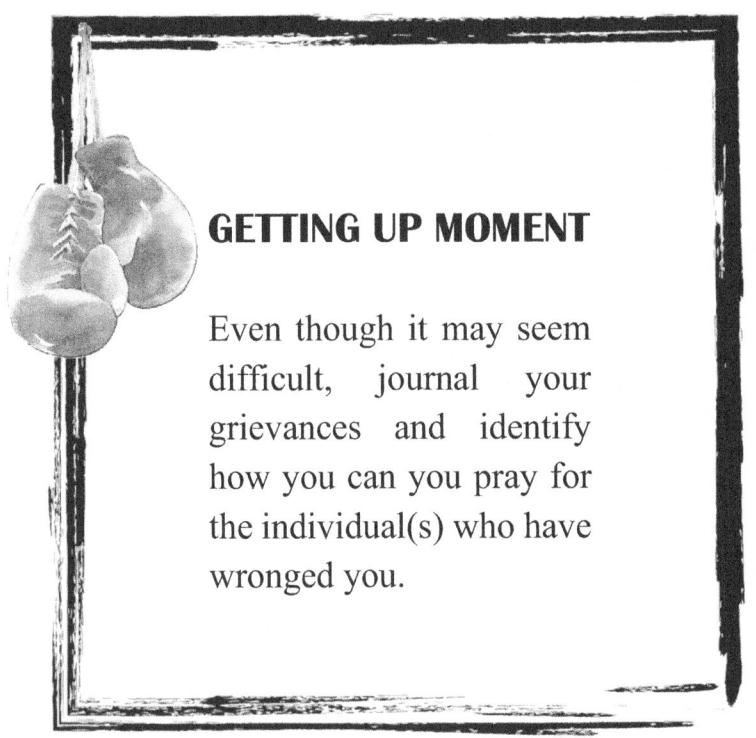

GETTING UP MOMENT

Even though it may seem difficult, journal your grievances and identify how you can you pray for the individual(s) who have wronged you.

-13-
WHEN IT IS TIME TO BE BRAVE...

A while ago, I was challenged to ask members of my inner circle what was needed for me to reach the next level to accomplish my dreams. Each person said the same thing, perhaps in different words, but still, a similar phrase. Everyone said that they were waiting on me—to be comfortable with me, to believe in me, and to step out. I was a little surprised at their candor. It's almost like they had been wondering if they would ever have the opportunity to tell me. When I opened the door of invitation, my loved ones swung it wide with passion and pent-up frustration. I assumed that I was waiting on God for the right timing, connections and circumstances. But then, I remembered all the times I got really close, only to hesitate. Always with the thoughts of, *"What if I'm not good enough? What if I can't do it? What if I fail?"* I was unsure of my ability and I was uncertain of God's desire to see me do it.

So there I stood in the same spot for a long time, paralyzed with indecision, inaction, and running in circles, while not gaining any new ground. I was in complete disbelief as I realized that fear of failing and complacency had converged on my life at the same time. Memories of unfinished projects and goals that had continuously rolled over to the next year invaded my thoughts. I had a million excuses for why these things were not complete, but the truth is it either got scary or seemed insurmountable.

My predicament may sound familiar to the first reaction of fear and distress by Queen Esther, when prompted by Mordecai to appear before King Ahasuerus, unannounced, to seek favor for the Jewish people. Queen Esther responded, in Esther 4:11 ESV, "All the king's servants and the people of the king's provinces know that if any man or woman goes to the king inside the inner court without being called, there is but one law—to be put to death, except the one whom the king holds out the golden scepter so that he [she] may live." I suspect that Queen Esther's confidence was shaken beyond imagination in that moment. We are no different. When we take our eyes off of the ability of our God, we are choosing to emphasize our human limitations. This distraction leads down a path of doubt and unbelief. Instead, we must shift our focus to the strength of God, being certain that our faith will please Him. In Hebrews 10:38 ESV, it states, "but by righteousness one shall live by faith, and if he shrinks back, [My] soul has no pleasure in him."

Yet, Queen Esther found her courage to forge ahead in faith. She bravely proclaimed in Esther 4:16 ESV, "Go, gather all the Jews to be found in Susa, and hold a fast on my behalf, and do not eat or drink for three days, night or day. I and my young women will also fast as you do. Then I will go to the king, though it is against the law, and if I perish, I perish." She was willing to assume the danger, believing that it was part of her God-given purpose.

Boldly stepping out is not easy. There is risk involved, and the potential for failure. I feared the humiliation that I associated with failure. It has taken a long time for me to understand that failure is, at times, inevitable and part of the process on the

WHEN IT IS TIME TO BE BRAVE...

road to success. Each time we fail, fall down, and get back up, we get closer to realizing our goal. For successful entrepreneurs, failure is not the end, but the beginning, because those episodes supply data points to fulfill their mission.

Just to be fair, I've experienced many successes in my life that required me to reach outside of my comfort zone. I suspect you have as well. However, if you are like me, there may still be an unfulfilled dream that you have yet to achieve. It may seem bigger than your own ability to obtain. I call them God-size dreams and they are usually scary and a little intimidating. Perhaps the fear is knowing that we will have to grow and develop in order to seize it.

The reason my friends and family believed they were waiting on me is because they saw someone ready for the next step, who had completed the hard work to train and grow in skills and competency. To them, I had what I needed to accomplish my dream. Were they correct? We will never know because I could not step out then.

So, what do we do when we know in our hearts that the hard work and training has occurred? It is at that exact moment we have to make the decision that it's time for us to fly. We are choosing to no longer dwell on the missed opportunities and failed attempts. Instead, we can determine to take the next best prospect and risk failure, along with success. There comes a point when you have to jump up and step out, trusting that God has got your back. By taking a chance, there is the possibility of mistakes and humiliation, but also success and great fulfillment. It will take courage and belief to pursue your opportunity.

At some point, the mama eagle knows it's time for the little eaglet to fly. So, she starts to make the nest uncomfortable. For us, the familiar just doesn't work anymore. We are no longer

GET BACK UP!

satisfied by it. When the eaglet is learning to fly, the mama eagle swoops in to save it just before it hits the ground. I imagine that is a terrifying experience for the eaglet, but it does not stop the flying lesson. A clue that it's time for us to soar is when the desire for the dream will not leave. "What happens to a dream deferred? Does it dry up like a raisin in the sun or fester like a sore?" This famous question posed in the poem Harlem by Langston Hughes has always been one of my favorites and is still relevant today. If we don't reach for the dream, it will gnaw at us and we will drink the cup of regret for what could have been.

Some dreams take enormous amounts of courage and are often very costly. I'm not necessarily speaking of finances, but rather emotions, perseverance, and tenacity. There are usually failures, denials, delays, setbacks, and any number of other challenges to overcome. But the passion for the dream keeps coming back. It won't leave. Yet, for those who endure to completion, there is a prize.

Close your eyes and imagine something that you have longed to accomplish, but it seems to always to escape your grasp—visualize it. Now, think about what's holding you back. Maybe you are like me and can think of a thousand reasons why you haven't reached your dream. Is it time to take a risk on your dream?

For me, I became more comfortable with stepping out as my confidence increased. Gradually I became more secure with my own ability, as I partnered with other people who already had a measure of the success I was seeking. They had jumped over many of the hurdles that I was trying to overcome. Watching them break through the barriers and learning their techniques encouraged me. Instead of aiming for a huge big goal, I focused on small incremental steps, which helped me to get unstuck. I was no longer paralyzed with fear. It is amazing how

WHEN IT IS TIME TO BE BRAVE...

teaming up with others, as we journey toward accomplishing our goals, makes it more bearable. Plus, we have our very own cheering squad.

There are no guarantees that the race will be easy. Most times not. However, it also helps to remember the love of the Father and that if God be for us, who can be against us? (Romans 8:31 NKJV). For days, when we question if God wants us to succeed, we must remind ourselves to trust Him more and believe His Word in Romans 8:37 NIV, "No, in all these things we are more than conquerors through him who loved us."

PRAYER

Dear Heavenly Father, I ask that You give my friends wisdom on how to start again and finish the purposes and tasks that You have for them. I ask for You to bring the people who will help them and hold them accountable. May they have a renewed sense of courage, peace and trust that You are with them to guide and protect them. In Jesus' Name, amen.

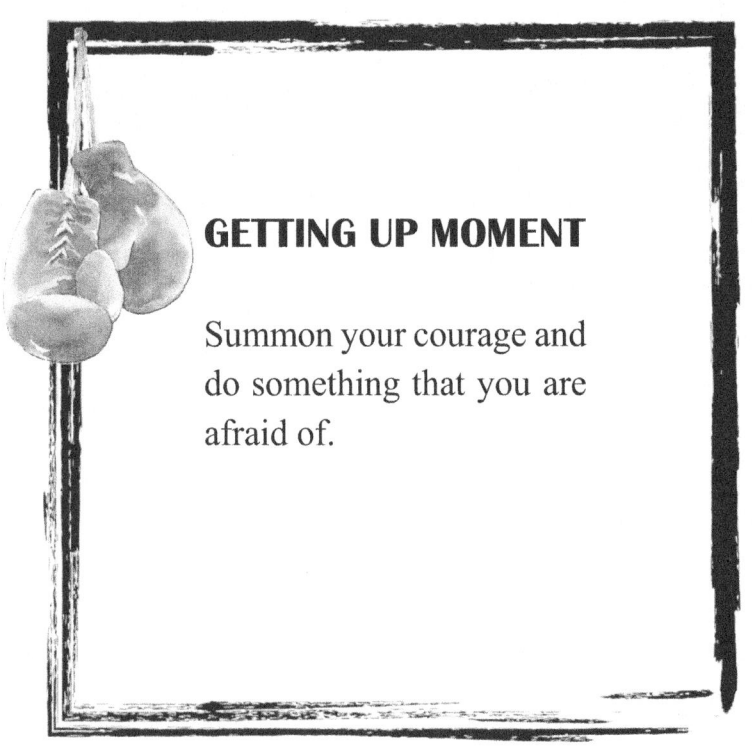

GETTING UP MOMENT

Summon your courage and do something that you are afraid of.

-14-
WHEN YOU FEEL BETRAYED...

Opening ourselves to love means that, on occasion, we will encounter heartache and loss. I used to fear those painful experiences. Honestly, I think I had a problem trusting people because I was afraid that they would betray me. I feared the disappointment and humiliation. I was aware of so many men who were not faithful to their wives. I found it troubling to trust someone who would later deceive and not come through when you were counting on them. There are times when I would hear about someone's spouse cheating on them. I couldn't help but wonder how in the world they were going to forgive. And my second thought, why stay in that relationship? I, myself, have also experienced betrayal in relationships and friendships. This influenced my ability to trust and connect with a mate. Instead, I retreated into my own safe world (as a commitment-phobe), but that's not living. Life is meant to be engaging and enjoyed.

    I realize now that many who have survived betrayal learned to live by a rule that I strongly recommend. I personally believe that it will lead to enormous amounts of happiness. We have to let people off the hook and give them permission to fail us. It seems rather negative doesn't it? And I must admit, a bit foreign to come from my optimistic persona; but the reality is that there are **no** perfect people. Some experiences suggest that there are mostly opportunistic individuals who take advantage of people and situations, but the vast majority of people just make mistakes. We have lapses in judgement and selfish tendencies. We are all a work-in-progress, and we mess up as we journey through life.

Have you ever noticed how some people get sidelined when they feel betrayed, while others don't seem to skip a beat? Maybe it is because one group anticipates there is a chance that not everyone who says they are in their camp is telling the truth or will remain there. It's kind of like that old saying, "I got your back…way back." We all need to pass this test, which I admit that I personally have failed many times. Instead of wanting retribution, when we feel abandoned and alone we should forgive, allow God to heal our hearts, and move forward to complete our work. When we open ourselves to love and forgiveness, we can experience the joy of community and relationships. It's like allowing yourself to experience both the storms and flowers during the spring season.

How do you bounce back after betrayal and disloyalty? The same way you do when you fall. You get back up, realizing that one or two experiences do not define your entire life. Truly, these disappointments could have a very small role in our lives if we choose **not** to magnify them. We can give these situations too loud a voice. It's about perspective. We must learn to handle our betrayals the same way as Jesus handled His—with love and restoration.

Jesus showed us such a great example of enduring the unfaithfulness and disloyalty from others. And not only with Judas. Peter is the disciple who said he would be with Jesus all the way. He cut off the ear of the solider who wanted to seize Jesus. He was passionate and completely devoted. Yet, he was

WHEN YOU FEEL BETRAYED...

also the man who denied Jesus three times, when our Lord really needed a friend.

Still, we see Jesus continue with His purpose. Jesus allowed room for Peter's humanness. Although Jesus must have been hurt and disappointed by Peter's failure to support Him, it did not stop the great work that still needed to be accomplished.

In the Gospel of John, Chapter Twenty-One, the miracle of the draught of fish is a demonstration of the power and authority of Jesus. The story emphasizes His mercy and redemption when experiencing unfaithfulness and failure. After catching a multitude of fish, Peter came to believe that Jesus was God, the Son. Peter left the fishing business completely, and did not return until after he failed Jesus miserably during the crucifixion and resurrection. Jesus used another miracle that mirrored the first (of the draught of fish) to remind Peter of the calling on his life. It is a beautiful example of God's love and Peter's restoration. We can apply Jesus' method to every area of failure, disappointment, and brokenness in our lives.

You can survive betrayal when you begin to understand it is simply part of doing life with other people and does not ultimately affect the outcome of your destiny. When we approach a breach of trust from that perspective, it loses power to control us. We are then free to love people for who they are and not what they can do for us. I often find it interesting how experiencing a broken relationship is like having a car accident. Stay with me. You could get lucky and not ever have a wreck in your life, but most insurance businesses factor in the likelihood that you will have at least one auto crash every ten years. Why? Because it is rare to drive every day on the roads and not have someone hit you, make a wrong turn, or get distracted.

Likewise, on the highway of life, there is the possibility of accidents in our relationships. It's just a part of existing. Some of those experiences cause a tremendous amount of pain and injury. We live in a world full of flawed people, including us. We all, at times, are blinded by ambition, selfishness, or greed. We lose our way, forget our commitments, underestimate challenges, and change our minds because we are not feeling it anymore—or just decide to quit. There are any number of reasons why we (you and I) are not faithful, dependable, and reliable. We're human. We have to let ourselves and each other off the hook.

I think about some of the moments in life when I have felt let down by people I trusted. I gave my help because I valued that person. There was a need and that is how I love people. I can remember times that I walked out faithfulness with tenacity, but I also am painfully aware of other times that I was the friend who was not reliable. And that's ok. It just means that none of us are perfect and, at any given time, we could be the faithful or the unfaithful.

I also had to learn that if someone doesn't want to be my friend anymore, then I can still embrace all of the other amazing people around me. One person's opinion should not be the dominating indicator of who I am. Part of the solution is choosing not to believe the lie that the devil is selling. A lone individual's unfaithfulness does not mean I lack value. That other someone may lack his or her own values or could not recognize my worth. Believe in yourself.

In order to move forward after a setback of betrayal, we must keep the right perspective. Instead of allowing ourselves to be stuck at a dead end, unable to advance, we must understand that it is a temporary challenge that does not have to derail our purpose. Someone's rejection of you is not a reflection of your worth, but rather an indication of what he or she values in life. I suspect that betrayal hurts so much because we feel, at times, that we could really use a friend and yet we are all alone. However, God is with us. It may be scary to open our hearts to

WHEN YOU FEEL BETRAYED…

love people again, but the joy we receive in return is worth the risk. The fear is that we will not be loved.

Divine love is not earned from our Heavenly Father. It belongs to us no matter our performance. It is actually more like we are adored. As Jesus told Peter to move forward with his purpose, we, too, have to move forward, whether someone was unfaithful to us or we were the one who failed. We must choose to be gracious toward each other as we understand Colossians 3:13 NIV, "Bear with each other and forgive whatever grievances you may have against one another. Forgive as the Lord forgave you."

PRAYER

Dear Heavenly Father, I ask that You heal every place that hurts for my precious friends. I pray that You would open their hearts to believe in Your faithfulness and love again. May You give them the strength they need to forgive and move forward. In Jesus' Name, amen.

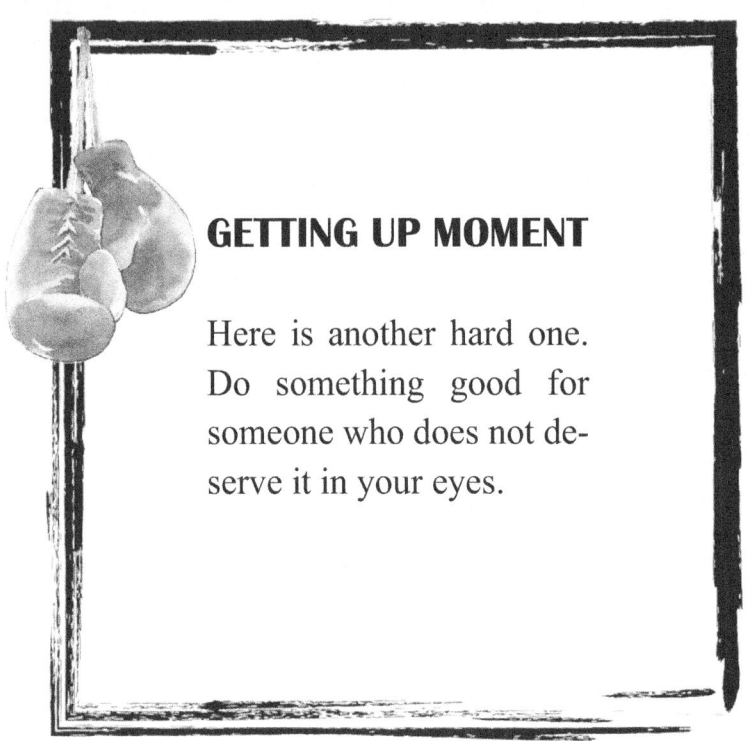

GETTING UP MOMENT

Here is another hard one. Do something good for someone who does not deserve it in your eyes.

-15-
WHEN YOU HAVE FAILED...

Getting back up is hard after you have failed. Most of us can think of something that we have failed in whether a relationship, project, someone, etc. Yet, there are probably just as many who can honestly say they have not endured a major failure. As the old saying goes: Just keep on living.

Finding your footing after a major failure is especially difficult. That is exactly where I found myself after college as a young adult. All during my undergraduate life, I spoke continuously to my family, friends, and probably strangers about my desire to go to law school and become an attorney. As far as I was concerned, it was a done deal. I took all the right courses. I completed the necessary internships in preparation. I picked out the law schools that I wanted to attend and I determined the area of law that I wanted to practice. I was ready. I dreamed of and visualized myself as an attorney. There was only one major hurdle standing in my way, which was completing the LSAT test for admission.

When I took the test, something went wrong. I'm not entirely sure what happened. My mom thinks is was the death of my grandfather during that period. The result is that the score on the admissions exam was horrible. It was so bad that the recommendation from the career counselor was to wait on law school and try again later or maybe pursue another career path. To say that I was disappointed is putting it mildly. I was devastated and felt humiliated. I had to face all those people who I had shared my dream with. Everyone in my circle knew that I failed at reaching my goal. I finally came up with a PR story like a natural, political, spin-doctor. The new script was that I had decided to take a year off and regroup because of the death of my grandfather. I'm sure Granddaddy was looking down from heaven shaking his head at me. With 20/20 hindsight, I probably should have just delayed taking the test. However, time off to grieve was never a consideration because I was so certain of achieving my goal. I just knew that I could not fail. After all, I had not really experienced failure at that point in life.

After practicing as an attorney for over nineteen years, I can assure you that no one cares about the score I made on the LSAT. In fact, no one cares about your score on the bar exam. The only requirement is that you passed and are licensed. I'm the one who decided that failure was dreadful and embarrassing. When I look back at that time after college, it was actually one of the best seasons of my life. I used the time to obtain my Masters in Public Administration (MPA), worked in health insurance, sold Mary Kay Cosmetics, and went to Laymen's Bible School at Agape School of World Evangelism. It was a beautiful season at home with my family and closest friends. So much of my success and balanced life during, as well as after, law school can be attributed to my experiences from those years.

Even today, I still benefit professionally and in my volunteer responsibilities from the skills I learned with my MPA. As an Independent Beauty Consultant, I learned about skin care,

WHEN YOU HAVE FAILED...

women's empowerment, business ownership, and sales in general. I know this has made such a difference in my life. As a Bible teacher, I am so thankful for the foundation that I received from Bible School during those years, as I currently teach in Women's Ministry.

If I had not failed in my initial attempt to attend law school, I would have missed all those wonderful experiences that are still blessing my life today. I see it clearly now. However, at the time I did not understand. Instead, I feared failure, what people would think or say about me, and the unknown. I had to believe Psalm 37:4 NKJV, "Delight yourself also in the LORD, and He shall give you the desires of your heart."

It looked like the end of a dream, but actually it was the beginning of a vibrant life. I also learned how to study for that particular exam. During that recovery season, I also realized that I truly wanted to be an attorney and it was worth the fight no matter how long it took me. I was ready to try again. In that failure, I learned a lot about me, my motivations, and my ability to bounce back from a setback.

One of the most valuable lessons to learn in life is how to lose. However, no one tells you that this means that you have to fail at something—and probably fail a lot. A successful businesswoman, many years my senior, once expressed this exact point to me. She encouraged me to embrace the opportunity of failure. I promptly told her that it is hard to become comfortable with failing when you are used to winning. Although winning is the goal and it feels good, it is in the failure that we learn the most. The lessons learned from failures are often the most valuable and remain with us for years to come. As painful as it is at times to endure, failures teach us how to lose and subsequently how to win.

GET BACK UP!

PRAYER

Dear Heavenly Father, I pray that You would comfort and instruct my dear friends as they experience failure. Lord, open their eyes to see all the wonderful opportunities You have for them as they walk through the disappointment of not obtaining their goal on their timeline. May they continue in faith believing that You will bring them to a flourishing finish. In Jesus' Name, amen.

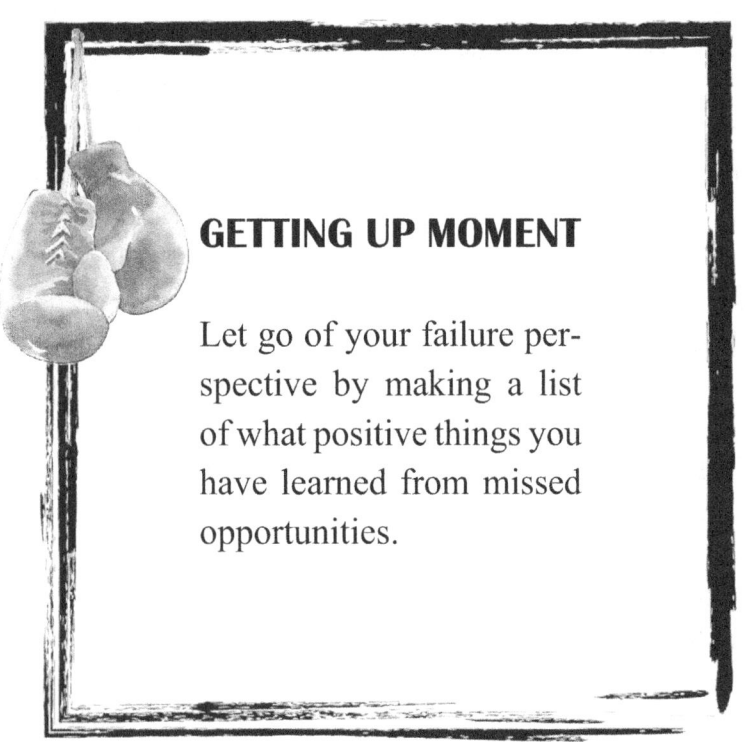

GETTING UP MOMENT

Let go of your failure perspective by making a list of what positive things you have learned from missed opportunities.

-16-
WHEN LIFE IS OVERWHELMING...

During the middle of a very busy day and an even more hectic week, the phone rang. On the other end was a dear friend who lived out of town. She mentioned the need to take care of some business early the next morning, in Houston, and asked if she could spend the night at my place—that same night. Although it was an unexpected request, and my house was not in any condition to entertain, I relented and said yes. I could hear the desperation in her voice. However, panic and alarm shot through me when she mentioned she would arrive in a couple of hours. *Lord, help me with the gift of hospitality please.* As my dear friend, and sister in Christ, sat across from me at the dining room table later that evening, I saw a stressed and overwhelmed woman who was at her breaking point. This was someone under extreme pressure. The kind of heaviness that causes you to crumble under the weight of the circumstances. I know that feeling, personally, when I have experienced situations that seemed insurmountable and continued much longer than I expected. I've also seen it in another friend who was caring for her elderly parents, both suffering with memory loss and mobility issues. That friend was once an accomplished businesswoman. However, she was stressed to her limits. Both of my friends were ready to give up.

We, too, may experience pressures that cause us to contemplate throwing in the towel. It's how we respond in those critical moments that make an impactful difference to the outcome. I have not always handled those events the right way, but I learned a lot from my mistakes. In the past, I would have a pity party and allow the demands to control my emotions. I can remember crying out to God, asking Him to help me with the burdens. In His great mercy, our Heavenly Father was always so faithful. Sometimes, it felt like I was in the fire just a little too long, but God is the Master Potter, as stated in Isaiah 45:9. He knows what He is doing. When the burdens and cares of life are mounting, we are safe in His hands. He also knows when our time is up on the potter's wheel.

During those times, God is strengthening us spiritually and building our character. We are learning to have stable emotions, regardless of the conditions we face. Part of that character building is growing in the fruits of meekness and patience. I've often heard it said we should never pray for patience because the process could be very long and painful. Likewise, the fruit of gentleness is usually developed under pressure. Perhaps, sometimes, we are in a situation because we are meant to be learning how to be restrained and tempered while we wait on God to rescue us.

In some seasons, there are numerous demands and commitments that can cause life to seem out of control. Some people have described it as holding an arm full of balls and knowing that if one more goes on the stack, they will all come tumbling down. In those times, when life's challenges are mounting, we must slow down and evaluate whether or not we are

WHEN LIFE IS OVERWHELMING...

trying to operate on our own terms and in our strength. In Matthew 11:28-29 NIV Jesus states, "Come to me, all you who are weary and burdened, and I will give you rest. Take my yoke upon you and learn from me, for I am gentle and humble in heart, and you will find rest for your souls." So, if we are carrying a heavy burden that is causing strain, stress, and overload, especially to the point of giving up, then we must ask if we are attempting to solve life's troubles in our own abilities, without God's help. Most of the time the answer is yes. The solution is surrendering control and the expected outcome to God. It is amazing what happens when we surrender. We are admitting that we are not able and do not have the capacity in ourselves to fix the situation. We are admitting that our circumstance is more than we can handle alone.

In our family, we love to play video and interactive games. When my niece was younger, she would get scared during one of the games. It would start to be too much for her. Then, all of a sudden she would say, "I need some help!" We would come rushing in full of passion and enthusiasm to finish her game along with her. I believe God loves to come in and rescue us in similar ways. God wants to be our hero and remind us that we are loved, treasured, and valued. When we surrender, it is the equivalent of saying that we need some help and may be in over our heads. Maybe it's time to say, "Help Daddy! I need your intervention or this is going to fall apart. I need your help to do this."

I'm not entirely sure why it takes so long for so many of us to ask for help. I suppose it could be pride, but more often it is just normal people trying to be strong. Only, I really don't think God wants us to be so strong. Yet, for some reason, we try to hold it all together on our own and without God. We have a God who wants to be our present help in times of trouble (Psalm 46:1 NIV). He wants to be in relationship with us. That is what it means to love someone. You help them. You come through for them. They are not perfect. They have made a lot of mistakes. But you love them anyway. Just as God forgave King David after his numerous transgressions and provided him with victory, we can be confident in the grace of God for us.

Learning to surrender all to our very capable Savior and believing in the Father's love requires trust. Trust is something we learn through experience, rather than from a book. As we encounter life's challenges, we eventually learn that we worship a God Who is reliable, and dependable. For some, trust is as easy as believing God when He describes Himself as faithful and trustworthy. But for many others, God proves Himself by showing His consistent, unchanging character. Growing trust takes practice.

Today, we often hear about the victory of people who once experienced a difficulty. Rarely do we hear from people as they are walking through the valley. The Christian life is not always easy. There is struggle, pain, and often unresolved matters that we must have faith to understand. I believe it is in those moments that our faith and trust in God grows and we mature in patience and endurance.

When I think about some of the times that I did not think I could make it on my own; I believe in those moments that God stepped in to rescue me. We have to trust that when life seems chaotic, God is still in control and delights in helping His children.

WHEN LIFE IS OVERWHELMING...
PRAYER

Dear Heavenly Father, I ask You to give my dear friends peace that passes all understanding. May they take comfort in knowing that You are loving, kind, faithful, and trustworthy. I pray that You would help them to surrender all their cares, worries and fears to You. In Jesus' Name, amen.

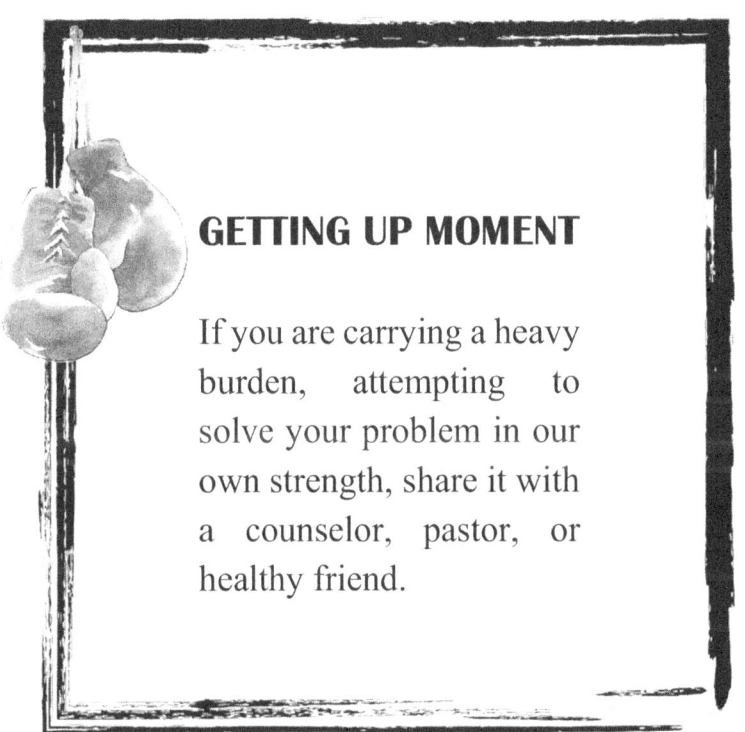

GETTING UP MOMENT

If you are carrying a heavy burden, attempting to solve your problem in our own strength, share it with a counselor, pastor, or healthy friend.

-17-
WHEN YOU WALK ALONE IN YOUR DREAM...

I still remember my first day of law school. I was so excited to finally pursue a long-term dream and a little anxious that I might not be able to do it. After all, there are a lot of horror stories about people failing their first year, experiencing breakdowns due to the pressure, or other major life events. As a first year student, I remember hearing that famous speech. "Look to your right and look to your left. One or both of those individuals will not finish law school with you. What will you do? Will you continue on or will you quit?" The speaker was challenging us to focus on the prize we were seeking and not on the behavior of our neighbors. He wanted us to chart our own course and not get distracted if someone else didn't complete their task. It turns out that the speaker was quite insightful. Many of my dear colleagues did not finish law school with me or even the first year. In fact, my two closest classmates did not return for a second year. I did so much with those ladies, from studying late hours, to praying together, grocery shopping, and church—we even lived in the same apartment complex.

GET BACK UP!

Although my thighs were thankful there would be no more midnight runs to Frenchy's for fried chicken, I was devastated hearing the news that they would not return for a second year. I was scared to face completing school alone, without my friends. I had to do exactly what the speaker had warned us about at the beginning of the fall semester. I was at a decision crossroad. Would I move forward after my dream without my cohorts or allow myself to stumble in their absence? That summer, I didn't see how I would keep on without them. I worried many nights about who I would study with, talk or pray with about the pressures of law school, and sit with at church.

In my heart, I had such a desire to be an attorney and I was not ready to give it up. So, I chose to persevere through that challenging season and continue pursuing my dream. However, I had to make a lot of adjustments to my life. I no longer studied late nights at the library; instead, I studied alone in my apartment, which I surprisingly enjoyed. I joined the Christian Legal Society on my campus and met many other Christians. I also met a married couple, a law student and his wife, who attended the same church as me. They often prayed with me and we shared many long talks about our faith and law school. It was so amazing how God met my needs during that time. He provided for every detail that I was worried about, as I continued my journey to become an attorney.

I had no idea that years later, I would have to call upon that same courage and tenacity learned in that difficult period of law school. This time I was leading a faith-based business and professional women's group at my church and my entire team transitioned out at the same time. I kept asking God if he was serious or if it was a joke. Sadly, it was not a joke. They were all leaving for logical, legitimate reasons—one moved out of the state, another changed jobs, and then the last one wanted to focus on her family. There I was holding the bag as the last

WHEN YOU WALK ALONE IN YOUR DREAM...

woman standing after twelve years of ministry. And yet again, I remembered the words of that speaker from law school, *"Will you continue on or will you quit?"*

Just as before in law school, I knew in my heart I was not ready to give up on the dream. I trusted God that the best days of that business women's group were not over. Being alone created an opportunity for new relationships and doing things differently. I believed that God still had more He wanted to accomplish with that group. There I was again, afraid to go it alone. But, this time I relied on God's faithfulness from the past. I wasn't really alone because God was with me. I could sense Him wanting me to be daring and brave. It reminds me of the courage we see in Ruth when she stayed with her mother-in-law, Naomi, after the death of their husbands, including following her to Bethlehem. With much conviction, Ruth explained her commitment to Naomi, in Ruth 1:16 NIV, "Don't urge me to leave you or to turn back from you. Where you go I will go, and where you stay I will stay. Your people will be my people and your God my God." I also had the support of my church's first lady and co-pastor. So, I did rebuild the team with God's direction and much prayer. I focused on how God helped me before, when I felt alone in those earlier law school years. I chose to believe that God would be faithful to rescue me again.

I thought it would be great to have a team half as good as the previous team and expected it to take at least a couple of years for authentic camaraderie. But God had other plans. He immediately brought wonderful, talented, spiritually mature women to come alongside me to lead our group. Although different ages, ethnicities, and talents, the new team had an instant bond and closeness. I'm so grateful to God for His provision and wisdom. We are now in our fifth year together and it has been one my greatest joys to work with these women. Together, we are passionate about the mission and our focus on the women, while striving to reflect Christ.

As I look back over that situation, I realize that I was hesitant about stepping into the unknown. However, that is exactly where we experience the "wow-factor" with God. As God describes Himself in Isaiah 55:9 NKJV, "For as the heavens are higher than the earth, So are My ways higher than your ways, and My thoughts than your thoughts." I was looking through my limited understanding of what was going **out** of my life, without perceiving the good that was about to walk **in**. I realize now that God could provide another amazing team that looked entirely different from the first team. They have their own gift mix that is especially created for what is necessary now. I suspect this lack of comprehension is probably the same way Joshua viewed the death of Moses or Elisha with the death of Elijah. After each loss, God had a new leader for His chosen people to complete the assignment. If we will let go of how we expect something to look, then we can experience a masterpiece creation from our God, the Creator.

As you pursue your dreams, there will be challenges, including moments when you are left seemingly by yourself to either continue or give up. It is in those moments that you may be tempted to turn back. Ask yourselves how bad you want it. It is the expectation of the vision that will help you to hold on through the struggle. As Christians, we sometimes do not acknowledge that there will be difficulty as we pursue our God-given dreams. However, this is **your** dream. It's not someone else's. You are the only one who has the desire for it. Yes, there are people who will support you and stay to the end because of loyalty or the same steadfast heart for the goal. But you, only, carry the vision and you will have to stick with it even when you are alone. There may also be many people who start the journey with you, but are not there at its completion. Although their contribution may have been impactful and valuable, you

WHEN YOU WALK ALONE IN YOUR DREAM...

must trust that their part in the dream may be over. It is at those times when we must be tenacious and determined to reach for our prize anyway.

PRAYER

Dear Lord, please give my friends steadfast faith to keep moving forward to accomplish their goals, especially when they find themselves alone. I ask for them to feel Your presence in a new way that would birth the confidence that You are leading them along the right path for their lives, taking care of every detail. In Jesus' Name, amen.

GETTING UP MOMENT

Write out a mission statement identifying your dreams.

-18-
WHEN YOU HAVE AN EMOTIONAL WOUND...

It started with a casual statement from my mother. "Your uncle phoned. He just got out of the hospital. He mentioned that you and your sister don't love him anymore because you never call and he hasn't seen you in years." I confess I was thinking of a million ways to end that conversation right away. But I was stuck. Caught without my next chess move. The uncle that my mom mentioned is not my favorite. He and I have never clicked. Our differences go back over twenty years, starting from an argument about his disapproval of me. By the end of that encounter, the die was cast and we were officially not on speaking terms.

I wish I could tell you that today he and I are close, but we are far from it. Our relationship has ebbed and flowed through the years. Although that particular encounter is a distant memory, there have been many others since. Each incident required its own meticulous navigation, similar to an acrobat walking a tightrope. It has been a truly painful experience learning to let go of the need to hold a grudge against him.

There have been times that I truly thought I had forgiven him and other times that seem to pick at the scab of a wound I was still trying to heal.

My mother asked me what it would take to move past this in my life. As I contemplated her question, many pensive thoughts flashed through my mind. An apology, perhaps? I wanted him to acknowledge the injustice. Finally, I blurted out that "I wanted him to stop acting the way he does. I wanted my family to hold him accountable for his actions." As we sat in the silence of the moment, I knew it was asking too much. The validation I was seeking would not come from human actions.

We don't get to control how God deals with the people who wrong us. The same love of God that rescues you and me, is the same love that pardons every adversary. It's a very sobering thought to realize that God loves the person who wronged us. I'm not saying there are not consequences or corrective measures for their actions. Only that they, just like us, are allowed to choose and receive redemption. We want God's forgiveness for all of our mistakes and missteps. Yet, our difficulty lies in accepting the fact that God has His arms open to our antagonist as well.

As time went on, there came a point when I made a decision to forgive, try to forget and move on with life. And it worked for many years. I can even recall saying a prayer for him every now and then. But when my mother asked me to call and express concern for him, I just could not do it. In my mind, she was asking too much and taking things just a little too far. Essentially, she was asking me to exhibit kindness and warmth. My mother wanted me to treat her brother in way that I felt he did not deserve. She was asking me to reconcile with him because **he** needed it. Imagine that. He needed me to be kind to him. To me, that was giving him permission to treat me the way

WHEN YOU HAVE AN EMOTIONAL WOUND...

he had and it was not right. That was unacceptable. The unrevealed truth is that there was something deep down in me that strongly disliked him. I know. I shudder when I admit it.

I rationalized those feelings away by saying it is possible to forgive and not have reconciliation. But if you cannot do something kind for a person, then the forgiveness is really surface level—and not complete. Through our original encounter, I suffered an emotional injury that was difficult to overcome. In order to rebound from traumatic personal history moments, we have to forgive completely. There is no way around it. The devil is so cunning and tries to convince us that we actually have the power to protect ourselves by putting up walls and holding onto offense. It is really a defense mechanism that shuts people out of our lives. The poisonous weapon we hold is not protecting us, but rather hurting us. The invisible wall is actually holding us hostage. It keeps the anger in our hearts and it does not allow God's love to heal and restore.

The reality is that there is nothing my uncle can say to give those years back to me. But God can redeem the time. Our Heavenly Father can bring healing and restoration to us from our painful experiences. Just as He did for Joseph, in Genesis 50:19-20 NIV, "But Joseph said to them, 'Don't be afraid. Am I in the place of God? You intended to harm me, but God intended it for good to accomplish what is now being done, the saving of many lives.' " Looking back, I believe those experiences completely derailed me because I was desperately seeking man's approval. That situation revealed my need to please those around me as a task for conditional love. Up to that point, so much of my identity was wrapped up in what people thought of me, especially my family. In the end, it really didn't matter because my identity rested in God, whether I knew it or not at the time. So what? My uncle and I disagreed on how to handle a matter and he didn't approve of my actions. The truth is, I am my own woman. I think a lot differently from him. My mother raised her daughters to be independent women with their own minds to think for themselves. It was a value that she wanted to impart to her children.

I am the one who magnified my uncle's voice in my life. I gave my power away to someone and let that determine **how I felt about me**. I believed all the lying negative words he spoke to me. The enemy was using this man's weakness to harm me. Through that experience, I began a journey to discover my true identity in Christ and find confidence in my voice. No one is to have that kind of control and impact on our self-worth. Not even our family and loved ones. It brought to surface a performance-based love that I had become accustomed to as a foundation of my self-worth. I recall a statement made about when "free-spirit" women marry or are born into the British royal family—they either bend or break under the pressure to conform to the family's way of life. I now understand that was what almost happened to me. But perhaps, there is another option—to grow into the confident, self-assured women that God wants us to be.

It is an early lesson in life that people fail you—they mess up. Likewise, we will fail people. That's just how life works, living with imperfect people in a fallen world. No one is perfect. There will be hurts and offenses doing life with people. We want to be able to dish out forgiveness according to our conditions, but receive it on a moment's notice. Forgiveness is releasing someone from a debt that they cannot pay. And we are in no position to withhold that from others. Mercy and forgiveness are not withheld from us. Part of the solution is to a make a choice based on obedience and being under the authority of God. The hard part is trusting that we serve a God of justice. He will make it up to us.

WHEN YOU HAVE AN EMOTIONAL WOUND...

Many of us will never get an apology or an acknowledgment of our pain. We may never get the satisfaction of seeing that person change their behavior. They may continue the abusive actions and yet we must still move on. We must trust in our loving God to heal all that was wounded, as we travel through life.

PRAYER

Dear Heavenly Father, I ask that you help my friends to forgive those who have hurt them deeply. Lord, heal their hearts of every emotional wound, especially those they have carried quietly from childhood. May You restore every broken place in their lives and give them beauty for any ashes they have experienced. In Jesus' Name, amen.

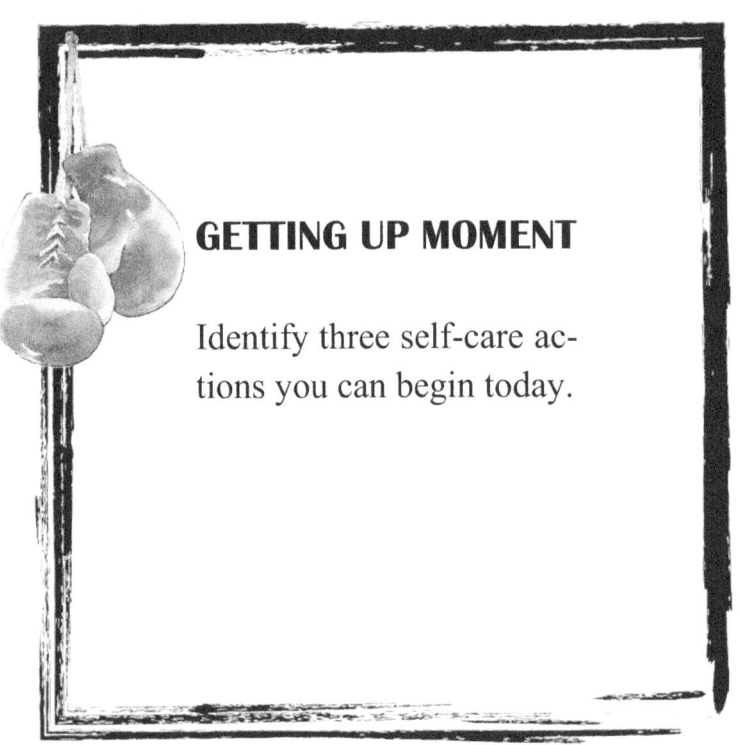

GETTING UP MOMENT

Identify three self-care actions you can begin today.

-19-
WHEN IT'S TIME TO REBUILD...

I'm not exactly sure why it took a trip to Berlin, Germany for me to learn how to trust again. But there I was in the back of a small store-front church, worshiping with tears and headphones as the translator sang with her whole heart. Some might call it a divine appointment. I call it a set up in a most unexpected place.

I was that girl who looked like she had it all together, but God and I knew the truth. On the inside, there was a heart actively processing disappointments and unanswered questions. *Ok, I admit it.* I'm the problem and the cause of my messy heart. A while back, I experienced a really hard season that extended for a couple of years. That particular season included a couple of health challenges, failed relationships, and a major conflict at work. It was a difficult season that caused me to question my faith and the loyalty of the people around me. Although I survived that time of testing, the scars remained and the doubts lingered.

During that period, I'd tell myself it was time to move on. I usually bounce back quickly. After all, there are goals to be accomplished, mountains to climb, and victories to realize.

GET BACK UP!

Only it's not that easy to pick yourself up after major setbacks, especially when we place ourselves on a pedestal with a dream to conquer the world. Somewhere between my love for reading and being the natural born, adventurous type, I was convinced it was my destiny to do big things and be somebody. I was determined to leave my mark on the world. From those childhood dreams to the ambitions of a professional woman, I have always held the heart of a champion, along with a resolute can-do spirit for success.

It would take years before I fully understood that life does not always turn out the way we dreamed it would. Sometimes, and quite often, we are disappointed or experience challenges. I confess it is still hard for me to even acknowledge that statement. This optimist and faith dweller still struggles to admit that the dream does not always succeed. What happens to the dreamer when she gets knocked down and defeat and frustration creep into the bones? Who is there to inspire and lift the encourager when she is discouraged and discontent? You may not like this answer, but she has to pick herself up and start over. We must learn to encourage ourselves in the Lord, which is exactly what David had to do at the battle of Ziklag, in I Samuel 30, when he returned to his camp to find it burned to the ground and his family taken captive. The Bible tells us, in I Samuel 30:6 KJV, "And David was greatly distressed; for the people spake of stoning him, because the soul of all the people was grieved, every man for his sons and for his daughters: but David encouraged himself in the LORD his God."

When the dream dies or we lose our way, we may have to go back to the beginning and dream again. Connecting to who we are and the passions that started our advancement is often the secret sauce of rebounding. I remember reading a story about the breakup of a famous Christian band. Like many, I was super disappointed they were no longer going to release

WHEN IT'S TIME TO REBUILD...

music or tour. Their melodies are still heard in churches all over the world. The front man for the band was asked what he intended to do next and to my surprise he said, "I'm going back to Sunday School." At first, I didn't understand his statement, but I realized I can only take it to mean that he was returning to the place where his passion for the Lord began. This particular music group had a successful career that spread over many decades. Although it was not mentioned specifically, I suspect that somewhere along that winding, long, and successful journey they experienced failure, challenges, and setbacks. A decision was made, at some point, to retreat and reset. That group leader was going back to the basics to rebuild.

When you're the idealist and the person everyone turns to for encouragement, it is easy to push down your emotions by putting an "S" on your chest to assume the role of superwoman for everyone else. But in real life, there are no superheroes. Instead, we are only flawed humans in desperate need of a dependable, reliable, and trustworthy God. Often sorrow and anguish hide in the shadow of our strengths and coping mechanisms. We think we are okay, and push through the pain, until it is unbearable. It's kind of like an ache in our bodies that we ignore until finally we can no longer walk or move a body part. It is only then that we are forced to address it.

Other times, it is obvious we are in distress because the residual effects of failure sneak up after long faith battles and unanswered prayers. That's what happened to my friend, Jessie. She thought she was in one place strong and faithful, but actually life's waves of difficult circumstances and challenges moved her to a totally opposite reality—sort of like drifting in the water without an anchor to still you. The worries and concerns of life had taken their toll on Jessie. Her strength was depleted, and she was unable to move forward. Even today, she is still struggling.

GET BACK UP!

That Sunday morning, in that small German church, I finally surrendered to the ache in my heart of not knowing how to rebuild my life or trust again. In that moment, I realized that like my friend Jessie, I had lost ground while weathering the storms of life. Then, I heard the preacher say something that I have never forgotten, "To trust people after you have been disappointed and let down, you have to start by trusting the Jesus in them." We can trust a loving Savior, who gave His life for us. Relying on Jesus seems so simple, yet it took a transatlantic flight for me see it. Of course, Jesus would know how to trust again. After all, he taught Peter to trust himself after denying Christ. Jesus did not let the journey to the cross derail His ultimate mission.

Sometimes we underestimate our strength level after difficult seasons. Once it is over, we are ready to move on. However, most of those seasons take a lot out of us. Even if you eventually obtain your goal or what you were wanting, you may find yourself exhausted physically, depleted emotionally, and weak.

Since I was a teenager, I have always enjoyed playing tennis. As an adult, I decided to reclaim my love of the game and take lessons again. Everything was going well for about a year, and then I over aggressively went for a ball and heard something snap. It was my knee or something close to it. This was a major setback for me because I was just about to begin playing in a league. Something I really wanted. After several months of allowing my knee to heal, I felt strong and ready to get back on the court. Off I went, full blast. I'm sure you can guess what happened next. And again, I heard something snap. It was not my knee this time. It was something else that caused me to lay up with a leg iced for several days and endure intense physical therapy. I was later told that the cause of the second injury was my lack of awareness of the current condition of my body after

WHEN IT'S TIME TO REBUILD...

the first injury. Basically, I had lost ground, physically, after my knee injury and I was not as strong as I used to be. Instead of going at it full throttle, I needed to take it slow. It is really clear now, but at the time, it did not occur to me that I was not my same strong self.

Rather than rushing forward, I needed to take the time to rebuild my body back to the condition I had before the injury. We have to do the same in other areas of life. After long fought faith battles, there must be allotted time and space for recovery. One of the first places to start is being honest with ourselves. We gain our footing to reform with awareness of our true condition and embracing our current location. When it is time to rebuild, but we are not exactly sure how because everything looks in disarray and scattered, then we must go back to Jesus. If it is learning to trust people again, then we must trust the Jesus in them. If the rebuilding is due to a personal failure, then we must trust in the love of Jesus for us, which is the same love He used to restore so many. And if the problem is that life has become so chaotic that it resembles the aftermath of a tornado, then guess what…Jesus is still well able to heal and restore us.

PRAYER

Dear Heavenly Father, I ask that You open the eyes of my friends to see and understand Your truth regarding their current situation. I also ask that You give them wisdom on how to rebuild and the courage to move forward. Lord, strengthen every weak area in their lives. May Your breath of life overtake them and cause them to recover from all that was lost. In Jesus' Name, amen.

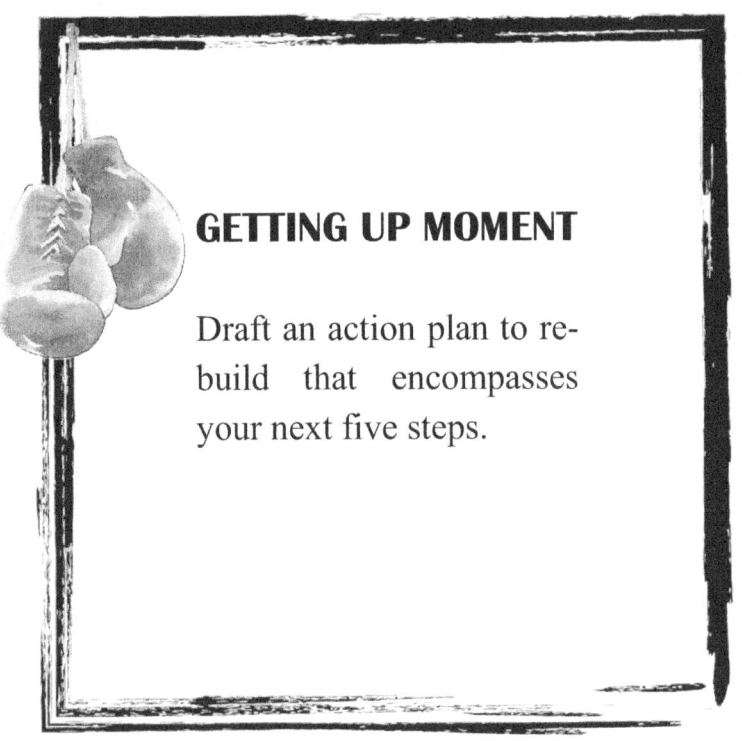

GETTING UP MOMENT

Draft an action plan to rebuild that encompasses your next five steps.

-20-
WHEN YOU FEEL UNWORTHY...

A good friend was on her way to my house to pick up documents for a community meeting. I could not attend because I was stuck at home with a sinus infection. The problem was not me being sick, but rather, that my house was in need of a little tender loving care. It showed the signs of a busy professional woman. *Lovely.* You see, I had been going through a rough time—stressed at work and challenges in my personal life. I was having a private pity party that I had only shared with God, until the moment my friend walked through the front door. I suspect she knew instantly, as she surveyed shoes in one pile and clothes sprawled on the couch. I will not bore you with all of the details, but we can just say "bachelorette pad." *My secret was out.* But all I remember is her kindness, and that I never heard of the matter in our circle of friends. I learned that day that I had a true friend who prays for me and did not judge or gossip about me. And it made me want to be a better friend to her. I also realized that I had been wearing a mask by pretending that everything was great on the outside. However, on the inside, I was an emotional bag of potatoes filled with pain.

GET BACK UP!

Perhaps one of the most freeing moments in our relationships is when we see each other in the clearness of sunlight, unable to hide or camouflage our flaws. It is moments like this that expose our real character and that of the people we choose to surround us. This ultimately allows us to live in freedom and to cultivate closer ties with them. Likewise, we discover the loving and compassionate character of our Father God when we have these same type of revealing experiences with Him. When we fail, His character does not change, but our understanding of Him deepens and becomes clearer. Understanding that God already sees us in truth allows us to rest in peace, knowing we are already loved, accepted, and approved—whether we do everything right or fail miserably. I hope this brings comfort to your hearts and eliminates the often automatic response to perform and try to earn worthiness.

No matter the length of time we live as Believers, many Christians struggle with the desire for approval and acceptance. It probably would surprise us to know that even those in ministry struggle in this same way. We assume they are deeply connected to God, and thus do not have self-doubt, insecurity or struggle to feel acceptable. I did not realize until much later in my faith walk that I approached God like an earthly father seeking His approval. In fact, I spent most of my life as an overachiever seeking external validation of my value, but not anymore. God has taught me to trust Him and believe in His approval of me through His faithfulness. His love is freely given, without conditions. God reveals His love through our experiences with Him.

For some reason, we trust God's love when we do everything right. But do we trust the Father's love when we miss it—when we fail? When we come to the realization that our sin is as red as scarlet, we must also realize that we are still loved. Yes, dirty, unclean, and in desperate need of a Savior, but so

WHEN YOU FEEL UNWORTHY...

incredibly loved. It was erroneous to think that we would live this life without an entanglement of sin. Likewise, it is flawed thinking that we have the power to clean ourselves from those same mistakes. Instead, we exchange our filthy garments for clean ones because of Jesus. And we follow the example of David, in Psalm 51:10 NKJV, when he asked, "Create in me a clean heart, O God, And renew a steadfast spirit in me." This begins a new walk and life for Believers. It's a new way of thinking that takes time to fully grasp. There is a renewal of our minds that must happen. God allows us to see our inadequacy without Him, so that we can understand our need for Him.

It is satan who tries to convince us that we are unloved, but it's just not truth. Unquestionably, we should not have the habit of sin, which becomes iniquity. Also, there are consequences for sinful acts, such as relationships ending or a scarred reputation. So, we should endeavor to live righteous, but understand that we can't live that kind of life without the Holy Spirit helping and empowering us. We can try with our best efforts, but ultimately it is not willpower that brings the victory. Living an upright life requires the power of the Holy Spirit. We fool ourselves into self-reliance, thinking that we can earn the Father's love. The gospel is free to us, which is part of the reason we call it the good news. Other than repenting and accepting Jesus as our Savior, God does the clean-up work. If we had to earn our redemption, or pay for it through performance, then it would not be a free gift from the Father.

There is something humbling and sobering about coming out of a pit of sin and knowing that you only survived it because of God. If He had not rescued you, then you would not have made it. This experience opens our heart to worship and honor our Father God with love and adoration. From the ashes of our greatest failures, a grateful heart with humility and compassion emerges in our lives. A heart of true worship becomes the foundation of our self-assurance.

In addition, a new confidence springs forth that is rooted in the security of our identities as sons and daughters of God. This new found certainty in God also eliminates people pleasing and living in fear of being rejected by people. We see a part of God's character that we did not really understand before. And when we come to the end of ourselves, after failing, it is then that we are free to experience the freedom of knowing that we were loved, approved, and accepted all along. We just didn't understand our true identity and inheritance of love.

Until I experienced God's love after my own failures, I had limited capacity to give and receive love. The Bible tells us to love our neighbor as ourselves. The catch is that we really have to love ourselves to love others. I had a lot of self-doubt and negative self-talk, and thus my ability to love others was crippled. I felt I never measured up and was always looking to be accepted. I was searching for love in all the wrong places, when actually it was right there, all along, exuding from my Heavenly Father. I just didn't realize that the acceptance and approval that I was seeking was already mine. There was no need for the striving or feelings of not measuring up. **God loves me just as I am and He loves you too.** There is such freedom when we realize that God is not going to abandon or reject us. Instead, He has already accepted and approved us. He is dependable, reliable, and faithful.

WHEN YOU FEEL UNWORTHY...

PRAYER

Dear Heavenly Father, I pray that my sweet friends who are reading this would come into a greater knowledge and understanding of Your love and approval for them. For every area of self-doubt and inadequacy, I ask You to replace it with assurance and peace. In Jesus' Name, amen.

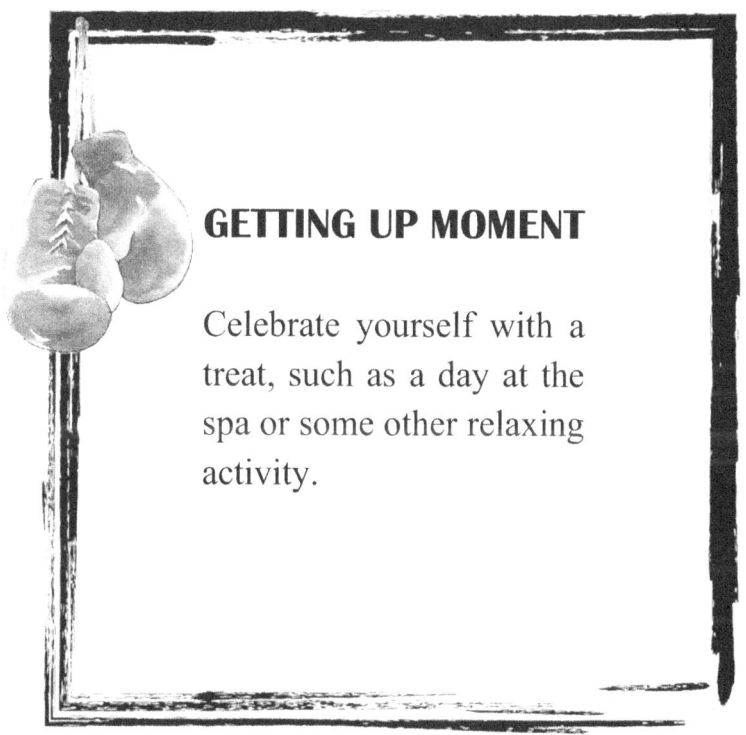

GETTING UP MOMENT

Celebrate yourself with a treat, such as a day at the spa or some other relaxing activity.

-21-
WHEN YOU CHANGE YOUR PERSPECTIVE...

I didn't see it coming. She seemed fine a couple of weeks before, at Thanksgiving. Although my grandmother was recovering from a recent injury, she looked like a normal, 80ish-year-old woman, suffering with Alzheimer's disease and living in an elderly care home. I remember asking God how long my grandmother would be in this condition. I didn't want her to suffer. Unknown to me at the time, my mother quietly inquired the same of God. I suppose this chapter could also be titled, "Be careful what you ask God for, because you just might get it." Two weeks later, my grandmother passed away and went to be with the Lord. Yes, she was saved, lived her full life, and I'm confident she is in Heaven with Jesus, but I still miss her dearly.

You see, I was Granny's girl. I have so many wonderful memories of our time together. Whether family vacations, our common love of family history, visiting graveyards, shopping, her doctor visits, cleaning her house, visiting the sick and shut-in, or church—I spent a lot of time with my grandmother. She was my childhood Sunday School teacher and first taught me about accepting Jesus as my Lord and Savior.

I always knew that I was loved and cherished by my grandmother, but not so much by my grandfather. He was not a man given to much emotion. He was the strong, silent type. Granddaddy went to work, loved to landscape his property, faithfully served in his church as a deacon and was responsible for the church building operations. At his death, over twenty years ago, I knew our family suffered the great loss of its patriarch and my grief was deep, but I could never really describe the loss—I was just numb. I'm not even sure I processed it completely.

However, the feeling was very different when my father died in 2011. Although we were in a great place, as father and daughter, when my dad passed, we were not particularly close in my formative years. Unfortunately, life did not afford me that luxury. More than anything, I believe I grieved what would never be when my natural father died. I just rationalized that I would be that girl who grew up without a daddy.

As my mom and I drove to the small town for granny's funeral, I began to replay moments in my life. Death has a way of forcing us to remember things long forgotten. The memories are not really gone, but tucked away. Sometimes they are neatly folded in a box in the back of the closet or in the attic. Other times, old memories are like a forgotten pothole in the road.

Something about the trip back made everything in my younger years look different. I began to remember very happy times. I was in such a hurry to follow my dreams, move to the big city, and conquer the world. I tried to run so hard and far away from home. Home had all the reminders of what I did not want for me. Yet, when I look back at all those photos from my childhood, I was so happy. I just didn't realize it. I felt safe,

WHEN YOU CHANGE YOUR PERSPECTIVE...

loved, cared for, and encouraged to excel, dream, and be fearless. Somehow I had forgotten that joy. I didn't understand, at the time, and I didn't see it. But now I do. When we are young, there can be a wrong understanding of what is really good for us. In my naivety, I didn't see the priceless value that was provided to me of a safe, loving home which was an incubator for my dreams. It didn't look the way I expected, but God knew it was the necessary fertile ground needed for me to grow into the woman I am today.

The enemy lied and I believed him when he said I was not good enough and less than. The truth is I did grow up with a daddy who was present in my life and was actually one of the best fathers in the world. He was a Godly man of integrity and love. He was very strong and a protector, but still kind and gentle. My granddaddy was dependable, reliable, and very trustworthy. And a girl could be so lucky as to have a guy like him for a husband. I remember a particular time that I needed to be picked up from school unexpectedly. He drove from his home, which was thirty minutes away, to pick me up, take me to my house, and then drive back to his own home. I realize now that the numbness I felt years ago at his passing was unexplainable grief due to the loss of my true father figure.

I struggled for years thinking that I had missed out on being a daddy's girl. Many of us think that God is holding out on us or keeping something from us, when the real issue is trusting what He has provided and being grateful. I never thought I was missing anything until I began to compare myself to others. It is amazing how we can be at peace if we keep our focus on Christ, instead of what is going on around us.

Often we look at what we don't have, all the while missing the blessing of what we do have in our life. When we don't understand what God is doing, we have to trust His character. In Lamentations 3:22-23 NASB (1995), the Word of God states, "The LORD'S lovingkindnesses indeed never cease, For His compassions never fail. They are new every morning; Great is [His] faithfulness." God is faithful and He can be trusted. There are so many biblical stories of God rescuing Believers from their failures and showing them undeserved mercy.

God is the Creator of the universe and Master Potter. We are not going to always understand what He is doing. It reminds me of a recent experience I had attending an art class with a few colleagues. Our job was to paint this beautiful, colorful forest with a backdrop of water and grass. I am not a painter and it was my first time in that type of setting. We started by painting the entire canvas black, which really did not make sense to me. Then slowly, the instructor began to teach us how to layer colors. At first, it looked like a huge glob of different colors on a black canvas. I assure you at this point, my painting did not look like a treasured piece of art. The strokes were inconsistent and unrecognizable. When it was finished, it was nothing short of a personal masterpiece. I was so surprised that my painting really looked like the colorful forest the instructor promised. In fact, it hangs in my office, and I regularly get compliments regarding it. I often gaze at my beautiful work of art as a reminder that sometimes the most breathtaking endings start messy and a little chaotic.

Just as I did with the painting, we all have to do with God. When we don't understand and life does not make sense to our human minds, we have to stick with Him. If we will trust His way, then I believe that we will see a beautiful, masterful masterpiece unfold. And along that journey, our perspective will change from that of a child's view to adult understanding, similar to the appreciation of art that comes from a faraway glance.

WHEN YOU CHANGE YOUR PERSPECTIVE...

PRAYER

Dear Heavenly Father, I pray that You give my dear friends a perspective that increases their understanding concerning anything that may be unsettled in their hearts. I also ask You to expand their trust in You and enable them to know with certainty that You are for their good and creating a masterpiece for them. In Jesus' Name, amen.

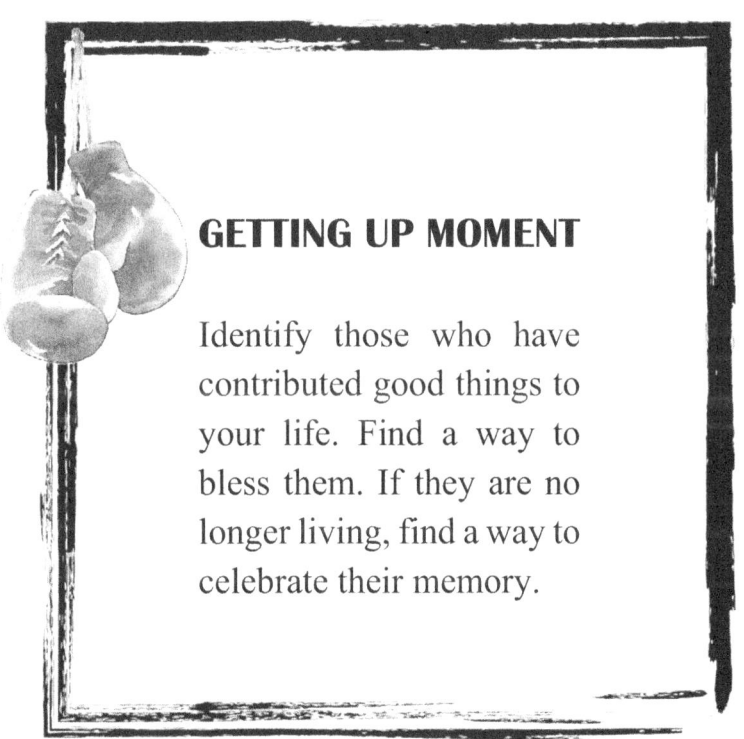

GETTING UP MOMENT

Identify those who have contributed good things to your life. Find a way to bless them. If they are no longer living, find a way to celebrate their memory.

-22-
WHEN YOU EXPERIENCE TRAUMA...

Living on the Gulf coast of Texas has a lot of advantages. For the most part, the weather is fabulous. Yes, we have our normal hurricane season that, as a region, we have learned to prepare and watch for. But there is not much during the winter season to concern us. At one point, I finally acquiesced that I didn't need all my winter coats from my days in Arkansas, a state which experiences all four seasons. Still, it was like parting with a childhood blanket to finally let go of my five thick winter coats (some of them wool) because they just were not needed in Houston and taking up too much space in my closets. After all, they were only used maybe two weeks out of the year. One, and at the most two, cold weather coverings was sufficient for most years.

Then there was this once-in-a-lifetime winter freeze that blanketed the entire state of Texas. Next, it was coupled with a very unexpected, added circumstance of the collapse of the Texas power grid under the intense demand by its users. Let's just say I was looking for every coat, blanket, and sleeping bag

GET BACK UP!

I could find in my home. No exaggeration, it caused an extreme amount of distress to most in the city. Many of my fellow Houstonians' behaviors and approach to the cold months changed going forward. People now own generators, who never thought it necessary before. Several friends transformed their wood-burning fireplaces to gas powered and others insulated their windows. There were many waiting weeks for a plumber to repair burst water pipes because of supply chain issues, ever trying to keep up with demand due to the storm.

That Texas subfreezing outbreak, with its power outages, grocery store shortages, and waterline breaks is an unforgettable, painful ordeal that to this day still have many questioning the reliability of the state's power grid. To put it bluntly, many experienced trauma from that event. *I know that I did.* This was a type of distress and injury from which we can see and understand the reactions. Yet, there are so many painful wounds to our loved ones, friends, strangers, and even ourselves that are not named or cannot be seen of the average passerby. From family genealogy beginnings, to the MeToo Movement and continuing to current time, more and more revelations of victimization and abuse surface. I personally find every story shared both heart wrenching and poignant. All traumatic encounters are different. They will not look the same. I've learned that trauma can be experienced in a multitude of ways—verbally, mentally, emotionally, or physically. Sometimes it's the pain of disappointment, failure, or an injury. Other times, it is what someone did to us. Perhaps, it is what we did to ourselves.

With all the hope and excitement of a new year a while back, I started off with water damage in my home. At the time, I had no idea it was the beginning of my entire life being flipped upside down. It turns out the water damage was extensive enough to require an insurance claim and a water restoration process. The much overdue repairs lead to a remodel of my

WHEN YOU EXPERIENCE TRAUMA...

outdated bathrooms.

As I embarked on renovating my home, I slowly began to realize that what I saw was a reflection of the condition of my life. Overflowing closets (needing to be cleared out) resembled my heart in need of self-care. The house had to be readied for contractors, which was no easy task. My home was in need of careful attention. And if I'm honest, so was I. Apparently, the Lord knew I needed reinforcements. He sent my mother to start me on the road to recovery. She was actually in town for a concert and a weekend getaway. But really, I think she arrived by divine assignment. My mom looked at my home and asked me what was wrong. I didn't know, but clearly something was amiss.

I didn't know at the time how to explain it. I just knew I was exhausted and depleted. My joy and my passion were gone. If you were to ask me how it happened, I'm not sure I could tell you. Maybe it was my toxic work environoment, coupled with poor boundaries at the office. There was that car accident a year before that lead to six months of physical therapy to walk without a limp. Or it could also have been my injured knee, from playing tennis six months before the wreck. There was also the death of my maternal grandmother that left a void needing to be filled, as well as my dear aunt's passing the following year.

Regardless of the reason, it had been a challenging and painful two years. And the reality was that there were many broken places all around me. Although my circumstances may be different from yours, there is a common thread that connects us. Experiencing trauma. It can mean different things to people, but its affects are similar. Trauma takes a toll on us and weighs us down where we can barely walk. For some, it is emotional or mental. For others, it's physical. Sometimes the injury is seen, but unfortunately, often unseen. Maybe the wound appears to be healed, but could still sting when touched. I believe this type of pain is real. I know my mine was. I don't profess to know every type suffering or to assign a value based on the severity level. I would never want to trivialize someone's painful experience. For each of us, our pain is profound. We are connected by our common bond of having experienced deep, crippling losses that many feel they will not survive. And yet, here we are...still breathing. Alive. Maybe crawling. Maybe crying. Maybe hiding.

How do we recover from painful, traumatic situations to find our footing during challenging seasons? I often think about when I fell off my bike as a child, and my grandmother sent my uncle to pick me up. I also can name numerous times that other people, even strangers, helped me through very difficult situations. Sometimes you need help to get back up. God did not create us to walk this life alone. In Ecclesiastes 4:9-10 NIV, it states "Two are better than one, because they have a good return for their work: If one falls down, his friend can help him up. But pity the man [or woman] who falls and has no one to help him [or her] up." A major part of our rebounding from trauma is seeking out and accepting the help of others. As we experience the compassion and fortitude of someone else, I believe our strength increases. It is really God's divine love flowing through a human vessel to us.

If you were to ask me the secret to overcoming trauma, I would say it is believing that God is for you and trusting in His love. We have to take to heart the words of Psalms 136:1 NIV, "Give thanks to the LORD, for [He] is good. His love endures forever." I say with empathy and humility that the recovery starts with a decision to trust in the Father's love and deciding to live again. It will be difficult. There may be a lot of clean up and some renovation that is needed. But just like my mother

WHEN YOU EXPERIENCE TRAUMA...

loved me through the reality of my then- current-status, God loves us even more in the midst of our ruins.

I can't really tell you how I fell into that pit. I just know that I was there and wallowed in it for a good while before I had enough and wanted to be free. It's time to come out of hiding and just surrender to the moment and our very gracious Lord. There is such healing in acceptance of the injury. I don't believe that God brought the destruction into our lives, but the reality is that He allowed the hardship. The journey is understanding that God will heal us from it and use it for a purpose and for good. It reminds me of God's promise to His people in Isaiah 43:2 NIV, "When you pass through the waters, I will be with you; and when you pass through the rivers, they will not sweep over you. When you walk through the fire, you will not be burned; the flames will not set you ablaze."

PRAYER

Dear Heavenly Father, I ask that You heal every broken place in the lives of my friends. May every place that was injured and hurt overflow with blessings and favor. And may that blessing extend for a thousand generations. Lord, I ask that You heal their hearts and restore to them all that has been lost. In Jesus' Name, amen.

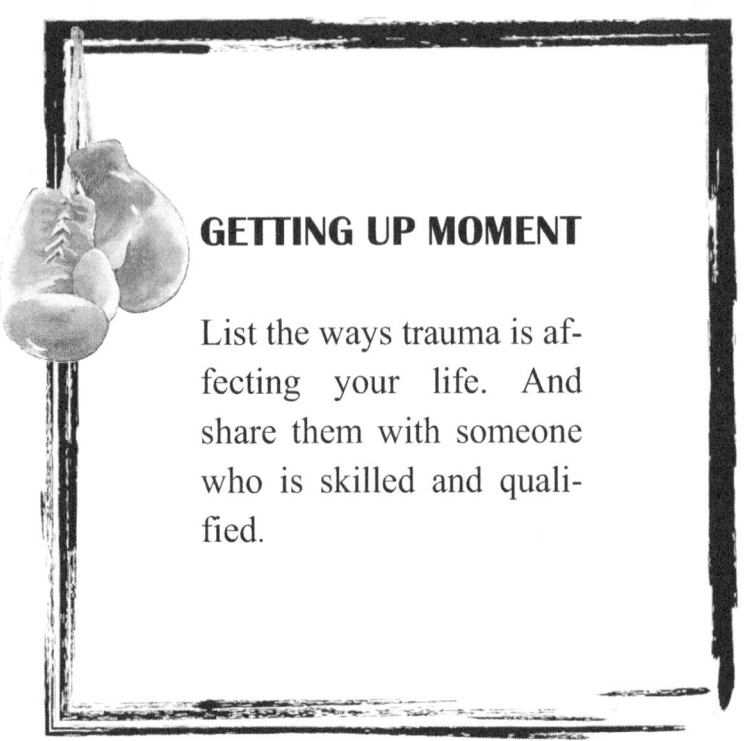

GETTING UP MOMENT

List the ways trauma is affecting your life. And share them with someone who is skilled and qualified.

-23-
WHEN YOU NEED A COMEBACK...

I often listened to friends and even encountered strangers who seemed sidelined and unable to rebound after disappointments or life-defining experiences. Some were mad at God, while others were stuck for a variety of other reasons. Yet all were unable to move forward. This also reminded me of my own struggles to regain my footing after a setback. The reality is that challenging times come to us all, but it is our responses that will determine what impacts they will have on our lives. As we navigate through life, we will experience many interruptions, obstacles, and detours along the way. We must decide if we will learn from the moment and grow to our next place of victory or if we will shrink back in defeat.

I have to confess that I am not naturally a person who enjoys a fight. As a youngster, my natural tendency was usually to run in the opposite direction. This is not the same for my family. I come from a determined and competitive sports-enthused kindred. In fact, both the guys and girls were often encouraged to participate in sports, including gymnastics, tennis, cheerleading, and swimming. While growing up, I recall one of my cousins playing high school football on a Friday night.

Get Back Up!

Most of our family was in the stands cheering him on. At one point, he was running with the ball and was hit really hard. He went down and the crowd was speechless. Then, my family could be heard yelling very boisterously for him to get up and get back in the game, as if he was Rocky Balboa in the flesh. I remember thinking, *"What kind of family am I part of right now?"* After all, this could be a serious injury, as sometimes are experienced by student athletes. Yet, in the spirit of a true comeback, my cousin got up and finished his game strong. Maybe that is why God determined that I needed this particular group of people in my life. I had to learn to hear that rallying call. When you get knocked down, you don't stay down. Instead, you have to get back up and keep going. It's called tenacity and fortitude. In other words, we have to develop the ability to bounce back.

But in life, you are either moving forward or falling behind. There really is no holding steady. When a season of difficulty arrives at your doorstep, you have the choice to either face it head on with courage or let it overwhelm you. It seems so simple, but I personally find it one of the hardest decisions in life. Because the truth is that some difficulties are so unbearable, and at times paralyzing, that it's tempting to take the easy way out and just avoid it.

However, that approach does not take into account that we have an enemy whose main goal is to "kill, steal and destroy us." What a sobering thought. This means that even if you live the most quiet, conflict-free life, you will still face trials and opposition because Jesus is your Lord and Savior. So, whether you like it or not, hardship is coming to you at some point in your life. And quite possibly, you may get knocked down when it comes. When you face that pivotal moment of decision, will you choose to get back up?

Although I have experienced various hard times in my life,

WHEN YOU NEED A COMEBACK...

I acknowledge that most of those occurred as an adult. To the average person looking in, I had a great life. Sure, I had the typical struggles of a middle class kid growing up in a single-parent home, but for the most part, I grew up in the blessing. It was not until I landed in Houston, Texas to attend law school that I began to experience true hardship for the first time. I remember when I could not pay my rent and I thought I was going to be evicted, and then God gave me such favor with the landlord. She kept extending the timeline for me to pay. At one point, I wanted to give up and go home. After all, that is what overachievers do when they can't handle life. But, I persevered through that hard season as a student. God used that moment in my life to teach me a lot about His character and faithfulness. I look back on that time and it seems like a distant memory. I remember it, but I don't feel the pain anymore.

I had many tests and faith challenges along the way after law school. When it seemed like I was not going to make it, God swooped in like a mama eagle and pulled me out of the trouble. Eventually, God restored me and turned my life completely around. But it was rocky for a moment and even the victorious ending was hard to envision. Through those tough, character building experiences, I learned that God will rescue you even when you give up.

We cannot predict the nature of our challenges or know about them ahead time. Instead, God is asking us to use our faith muscles to power through to the end. We may not always understand or agree with how God is allowing a situation to unfold, but we can expand those muscles by acknowledging that God is on our side. He is fighting for us. He is faithful, merciful, and gracious. He is kind. His power is unmatched. And He is a God of justice. The Word of God states, in Isaiah 61:8 NLT, "For I, the LORD, love justice. I hate robbery and wrongdoing. I will faithfully reward my people for their suffering and make an everlasting covenant with them." In fact, it has been my trust in God's love for justice that has sustained me through life's deepest disappointments.

Some hardships occur because we messed up, whether through sin, bad judgement, or any number of other personal failures. Other battles are because someone else failed. Then, there are experiences that are just a part of life. The Word of God describes this concept in Matthew 5:45 NKJV, as raining on the just and the unjust. However, as Believers we must continue to move forward as we live by faith. The twists, turns, setbacks, or trials may not make sense to our natural minds. Our job is to believe and fight the good fight of faith. Regardless of the circumstance and how it looks, we have to know deep inside that we are more than conquerors, as described in Romans 8:37 NIV, "No, in all these things we are more than conquerors through him who loved us." And remind ourselves, "Now Thanks be to God, who always causes us in triumph in Christ..." 2 Cor. 2:14 NKJV. So, it's not over until we win.

You will get back up from every setback and live to fight again as you strengthen your faith and resolve to persevere through challenges. Let there be no misunderstanding. Champions get back up. They always comeback. My hope is that you will be encouraged to try again, believe again, and live again after your own difficult moments. After all, I love a good comeback story and would love to hear yours. At the end of the day, you are a champion because God has called you for that purpose. And don't forget that you have a great cloud of witnesses in heaven cheering you on.

WHEN YOU NEED A COMEBACK...

PRAYER

Dear Heavenly Father, I pray for my dear friends to have a renewed passion to pursue Your purpose for their lives. Lord, I ask You to give them tenacity, joy, and fortitude to finish strong. May You help them to pursue and recover all that they have lost through setbacks and disappointments. In Jesus' Name, amen.

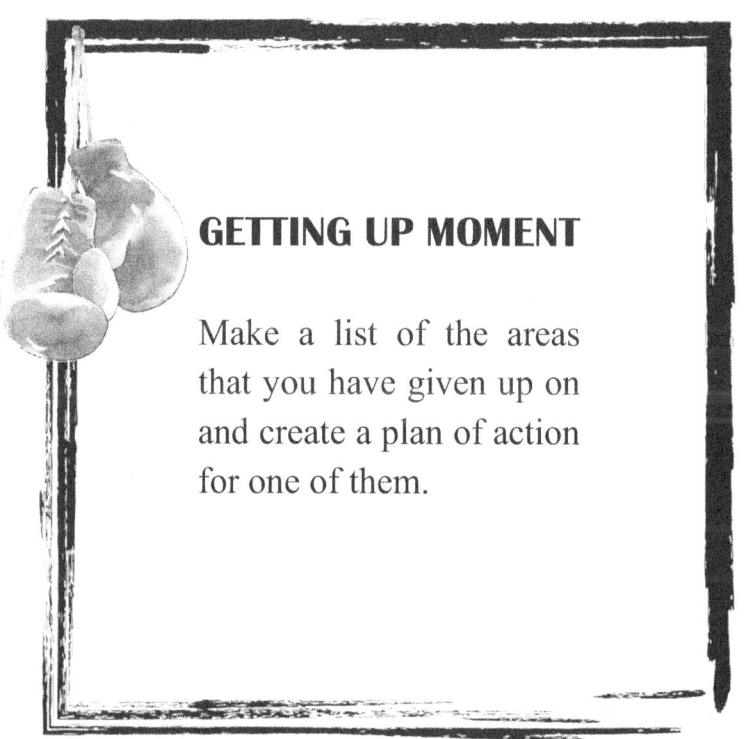

GETTING UP MOMENT

Make a list of the areas that you have given up on and create a plan of action for one of them.

-24-
WHEN IT'S TIME TO BEGIN AGAIN...

Most of us have fallen off a bike or taken a tumble causing an injury. And some of those cuts and bruises can take a long time to heal and become a scar. Sometimes, they remain fresh and very tender for a long while. The goal is to give that wound time and space to recover. I was always that child whose mother constantly reminded her not to pick at the scab. My mother would insist the sore was in the healing process. Likewise, there are some experiences in life that leave a gaping hole of hurt in our hearts. We fall down in relationships, business, health, and so many other areas. There is an injury. It hurts. But then, we must collect ourselves, rise to our feet, and move forward.

    You are probably thinking that is really tough love. Let's just admit that it is the getting up and taking the next step that is often really difficult, yet so very pivotal at the same time. I once had a supervisor who loved to say, "Nicole, turn the page." It took me a really long time to finally understand. She was saying that sometimes bad things happen to us that boggle

GET BACK UP!

the mind. As much as we try to figure it out or understand the cause, we cannot. When we experience those situations we have to learn to move on and start again. The "new page" she was referring to is a blank canvas we can create without any baggage from the previous encounter. In other words, we must choose to not let those negative experiences derail our advancement. We have to journey on, not ever understanding why we endured some situations and leave them unresolved. This pressing on may include rebuilding a business, forgiving a friend, or leaving a job. It reminds me of those unsolved cases in thousands of crime labs across the country. We are trusting that God will use those conditions for our good. As we continue on, we believe that He will heal and reconcile us.

This is not the easiest task for me either. Holding on with tenacity and persevering is the bedrock of my dreamer's heart; however, the reality is that sometimes we have to let go and reclaim our joy. I still remember when I finally decided it was time to leave a very stressful and demanding job. I loved the people. I was inspired by the vision and the bold mission. I wanted to stick it out. I had designed goals and tasks to help achieve so much at the organization. I really wanted to make it work. But that job had taken more withdrawals than I personally received in deposits. My energy was depleted and I had nothing left to give that company. To some it may have seemed like I was giving up or throwing in the towel. However, I choose to say I evaluated whether that environment deserved my continued resources. I had to come to realize that the energy used to sustain that challenge was needed to advance the purpose and plans that God had for me. Is it the same for you? Letting go of the fight allows the good to enter your life.

I have this favorite bathroom stop whenever I drive to Little Rock from Houston. I noticed on the last trip that it was starting to look a little run down. Okay, a lot. I realized that I

WHEN IT'S TIME TO BEGIN AGAIN…

was going to have to find another stop. At first, it seemed like there were no other viable options. I looked on the map and online. I didn't see another good place. Yes, I will admit it. I'm very particular in my bathroom stops. On the drive back, I asked the Lord to help me find a new stop that was safe and clean. To my surprise there were two or three really good stops at the junction where I change highways. I had never seen them before. It was as if they magically appeared. What changed? I changed. I was finally open to the new. I was no longer fixated on my current predicament.

I really think it is the same way for us. I can't tell you the number of times that friends shared that when they finally decided to leave a horrible job, a multitude of new opportunities appeared. Or, when they ended a bad relationship, God sent the one for them to marry. I believe the issue is that they were eventually open to receiving and enjoying something new. The Word of God states, in Isaiah 43:19 KJV, "Behold, I will do a new thing, Now it shall spring forth; Shall you not know it? I will even make a road in the wilderness and rivers in the desert." To experience the joy and restoration we seek, it often means we have embrace the "new thing" that God wants to do in us, through us, and for us.

Another way of looking at this concept is to think of shifting from surviving to thriving. I'm asking you to give yourself permission to shine. This requires you to let go of the painful, unimaginable that may have happened to you. Instead, believe that God has so much more in your future if you will keep going. It is kind of like that old tale about the dog that was moaning so loud because he was laying on a nail. When the owner was asked why the dog does not move, the owner replied that the nail did not hurt enough.

There is something that happens to the soul when we finally decide we are ready to move on and let go. Undeniably, the pain was real. Maybe you gave it your all and it just didn't work out. Now, is the time to trust God with the results. The moment has come to release your fist and grab hold of your dreams. When I look back at the job I left, I actually benefited a great deal from being there. It was difficult and challenging, yet I'm a better lawyer because of that job. I'm also more tech savvy, a consummate team player, and I know more about what I want. The truth is that I learned a lot about me in that difficulty. I grew in ways I never thought possible. And then I moved on to the next place of provision and supply that God determined was for me. I urge you not to allow failures or missteps to hinder your progress. There will be times that we have to "turn the page" and start again. We can trust that there is so much more good to come. We can also believe that there is an abundance of joy on the way.

WHEN IT'S TIME TO BEGIN AGAIN...

PRAYER

Dear Heavenly Father, I ask that You heal my dear friends from those hurtful experiences that have been difficult for them to release. I pray that You would give them the grace and strength to let go of negative mindsets from the past. May they have wisdom as they rebuild every broken wall in their lives. Lord, I ask You to restore joy to their hearts. In Jesus' Name, amen.

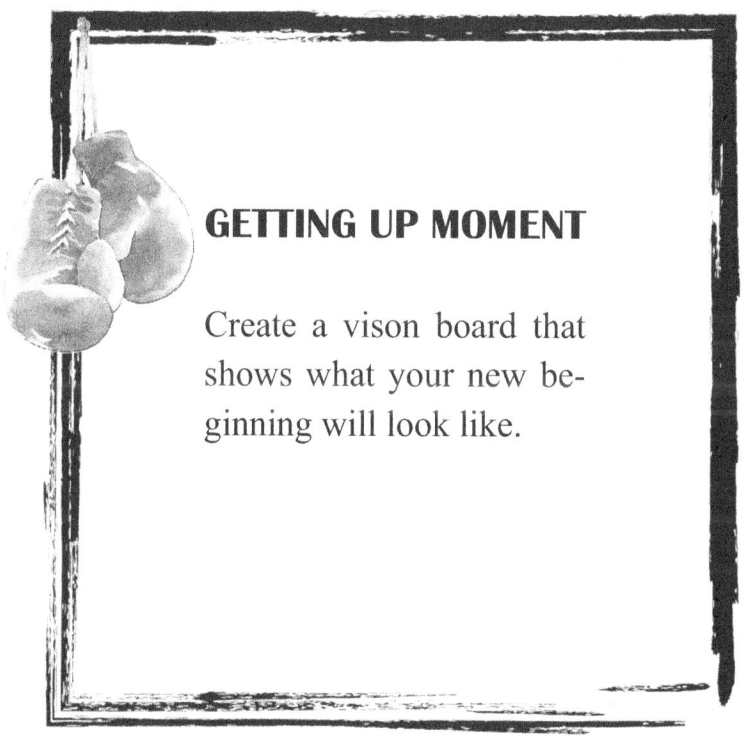

GETTING UP MOMENT

Create a vison board that shows what your new beginning will look like.

AUTHOR BIO

Nicole Montgomery is an attorney, conference speaker, and author. She is passionate about inspiring others to reach for their dreams and to live beautiful, enriched, and vibrant lives.

For over a decade, Nicole has led a women's faith-based professional and business ministry that has impacted the lives of thousands of women. Additionally, Nicole loves the Word of God and is a prolific Bible teacher. Nicole enjoys speaking regularly at both her local church and other venues.

Get Back Up! Overcoming the Hard Moments in Life is Nicole's first offering as an author; however, she is looking forward to releasing new titles in the future. Her previous publishing credits are in the devotional genre. You can subscribe to Nicole's newsletter at www.NicoleMontgomery.com. She would love to hear from you!

GET BACK UP! SCRIPTURES

Psalms 37:23-24 NIV
"The Lord makes firm the steps of the one who delights in him; though he may stumble, he will not fall, for the Lord upholds him with His hand."

2 Corinthians 2:14 NKJV
"Now thanks be to God who always leads us in triumph in Christ, and through us diffuses the fragrance of His knowledge in every place."

Genesis 18:14 NIV
"Is anything too hard for the Lord? I will return to you at the appointed time next year, and Sarah will have a son."

Before We Begin

John 16:33 NLT
"I have told you all this so that you may have peace in me. Here on earth you will have many trials and sorrows. But take heart, because I have overcome the world."

Chapter 1: When You Want To Give Up...

Isaiah 61:3 NIV
"...provide for those who grieve in Zion—to bestow on them a crown of beauty instead of ashes, the oil of joy instead of mourning, and a garment of praise instead of a spirit of despair. They will be called oaks of righteousness, a planting of the Lord for the display of his splendor."

GET BACK UP! SCRIPTURES

HEBREWS 12:1-2 ESV

"Therefore, since we are surrounded by so great a cloud of witnesses, let us also lay aside every weight, and sin which clings so closely, and let us run with endurance the race that is set before us, looking to Jesus, the founder and perfecter of our faith, who for the joy that was set before him endured the cross, despising the shame, and is seated at the right hand of the throne of God."

CHAPTER 2: WHEN YOU ARE AFRAID...

2 TIMOTHY 1:7 NKJV

"For God has not given us a spirit of fear, but of power and of love and of a sound mind."

ZECHARIAH 2:8 NKJV

"...for he who touches you touches the apple of His eye."

ISAIAH 49:16 NKJV

"See, I have inscribed you on the palms of My hands; Your walls are continually before Me."

MATTHEW 14:28-29 ESV

"And Peter answered him, 'Lord, if it is you, command me to come to you on the water.' He said, 'Come.' So Peter got out of the boat and walked on the water and came to Jesus."

MATTHEW 28:20 NLT

"...And be sure of this, I am with you always, even to the end of the age."

CHAPTER 3: WHEN YOU EXPERIENCE A HEALTH CRISIS...

PSALM 18:32-33 NKJV

"It is God who arms me with strength, And makes my way

perfect. He makes my feet like the feet of deer, And sets me on my high places."

PSALM 23:4 NKJV
"Yea, though I walk through the valley of the shadow of death, I will fear no evil; For You are with me; Your rod and Your staff, they comfort me."

PSALM 23:1-3 NKJV
"The Lord is my shepherd; I shall not want. He makes me to lie down in green pastures; He leads beside the still waters. He restores my soul; He leads me in the paths of righteousness for His name's sake."

CHAPTER 4: WHEN YOU NEED A NEW SELF-IMAGE...

JUDGES 6:15 ESV
..."Please, Lord, how can I save Israel? Behold, my clan is the weakest in Manasseh, and I am the least in my father's house."

JUDGES 6:12 ESV
"And the angel of the Lord appeared to him and said to him, 'The Lord is with you, O mighty man of valor.'"

MARK 12:31 NIV
"The second is this: 'Love your neighbor as yourself.' There is no commandment greater than these."

JOHN 3:16-17 NLT
" For this is how God loved the world: He gave his one and only Son, so that everyone who believes in him will not perish but have eternal life. God sent his Son into the world not to judge the world, but to save the world through him."

GET BACK UP! SCRIPTURES

EPHESIANS 2:10 NLT
"For we are God's masterpiece. He has created us anew in Christ Jesus, so we can do the good things he planned for us long ago."

CHAPTER 5: WHEN YOUR FAITH IS SHIPWRECKED...

MATTHEW 8:26 NLT
"Jesus responded, 'Why are you afraid? You have so little faith!' Then He got up and rebuked the wind and waves, and suddenly there was a great calm."

CHAPTER 6: WHEN YOU FEEL LOST...

PSALM 119:105 NKJV
"Your word is a lamp to my feet And a light to my path."

PSALM 27:11 NLT
"Teach me how to live, O LORD. Lead me along the right path, for my enemies are waiting for me"

PSALM 119:105 NKJV
"Your word *is* a lamp to my feet And a light to my path"

PROVERBS 8:2-3 NKJV
"[Wisdom] takes her stand on the top of the high hill, beside the way, where the paths meet. She cries out by the gates, at the entry of the city, at the entrance of the doors:"

ZECHARIAH 1:3 NKJV
"Therefore say to them, 'Thus says the Lord of hosts: "Return to Me," says the Lord of hosts, "and I will return to you," says the Lord of hosts.' "

MATTHEW 7:11 NLT

"So if you sinful people know how to give good gifts to your children, how much more will your heavenly Father give good gifts to those who ask him."

CHAPTER 7: WHEN YOU ARE SINGLE LATE IN LIFE...

GENESIS 3:11 NKJV

"...'Who told you that you were naked? Have you eaten from the tree of which I commanded you that you should not eat?'"

PROVERBS 3:5-6 NKJV

"Trust in the Lord with all your heart, and lean not on your own understanding; In all your ways acknowledge Him, and He shall direct your paths."

PHILIPPIANS 1:6 MSG

"There has never been the slightest doubt in my mind that the God who started this great work in you would keep at it and bring it to a flourishing finish on the very day Christ Jesus appears."

PHILIPPIANS 4:11-13 TPT

"I'm not telling you this because I'm in need, for I have learned to be satisfied in any circumstance. I know what it means to lack, and I know what it means to experience overwhelming abundance. For I'm trained in the secret of overcoming all things, whether in fullness or in hunger. And I find that the strength of Christ's explosive power infuses me to conquer every difficulty."

2 CORINTHIANS 12:9 NKJV

"And He said to me, 'My grace is sufficient for you, for My strength is made perfect in weakness.' Therefore most gladly I will rather boast in my infirmities, that the power of Christ may rest upon me."

Chapter 8: When You Feel Forgotten...

2 Peter 1:5-6 NIV

"For this very reason, make every effort to add to your faith goodness; and to goodness, knowledge; and to knowledge, self-control; and to self-control, perseverance; and to perseverance, godliness;"

Daniel 6:22 NKJV

"My God sent His angel and shut the lions' mouths, so that they have not hurt me, because I was found innocent before Him; and also, O king, I have done no wrong before you."

Joshua 1:9 NKJV

"Have I not commanded you? Be strong and of good courage; do not be afraid, nor be dismayed, for the Lord your God is with you wherever you go."

Chapter 9: When It's Time To Fight...

1 Peter 5:8 NKJV

"Be sober, be vigilant; because your adversary the devil walks about like a roaring lion, seeking whom he may devour."

Jeremiah 29:11 NIV

"For I know the plans I have for you," declares the Lord, "plans to prosper you and not to harm you, plans to give you hope and a future."

Ephesians 6:13 NIV

"Therefore put on the full armor of God, so that when the day of evil comes, you may be able to stand your ground, and after you have done everything, to stand."

Chapter 10: When It's Time For A Change...

JEREMIAH 33:3 ESV
"Call to me and I will answer you, and will tell you great and hidden things that you have not known."

PSALMS 16:11 ESV
"You make known to me the path of life; in your presence there is fullness of joy; at your right hand are pleasures forevermore."

Chapter 11: When You Take Steps Of Faith...

NUMBERS 13:33 KJV
"And there we saw the giants, the sons of Anak, which come of the giants: and we were in our own sight as grasshoppers, and so we were in their sight."

JOSHUA 3:8 NIV
"Tell the priests who carry the ark of the covenant: 'when you reach the edge of the Jordan's waters, go and stand in the river.' "

HEBREWS 13:6 NKJV
"...The Lord is my helper; I will not fear. What can man do to me?"

Chapter 12: When You Are Tempted To Hate...

JAMES 1:2-3 NKJV
"My brethren, count it all joy when you fall into various trials, knowing that the testing of your faith produces patience. But let patience have its perfect work, that you may be perfect

and complete, lacking nothing."

HEBREWS 11:6 NKJV

"But without faith it is impossible to please Him, for he who comes to God must believe that He is, and that He is a rewarder of those who diligently seek Him."

CHAPTER 13: WHEN IT'S TIME TO BE BRAVE...

ESTHER 4:11 ESV

"All the king's servants and the people of the king's provinces know that if any man or woman goes to the king inside the inner court without being called, there is but one law—to be put to death, except the one whom the king holds out the golden scepter so that he [she] may live."

ESTHER 4:16 ESV

" 'Go, gather all the Jews to be found in Susa, and hold a fast on my behalf, and do not eat or drink for three days, night or day. I and my young women will also fast as you do. Then I will go to the king, though it is against the law, and if I perish, I perish.' "

ROMANS 8:31 NKJV

"What then shall we say to these things? If God is for us, who can be against us?"

ROMANS 8:37 NIV

"No, in all these things we are more than conquerors through him who loved us."

CHAPTER 14: WHEN YOU FEEL BETRAYED...

COLOSSIANS 3:13 NIV

"Bear with each other and forgive whatever grievances

you may have against one another. Forgive as the Lord forgave you."

CHAPTER 15: WHEN YOU HAVE FAILED...

PSALM 37:4 NKJV
"Delight yourself also in the LORD, and He shall give you the desires of your heart."

CHAPTER 16: WHEN LIFE IS OVERWHELMING...

MATTHEW 11:28-29 NIV
"Come to me, all you who are weary and burdened, and I will give you rest. Take my yoke upon you and learn from me, for I am gentle and humble in heart, and you will find rest for your souls."

PSALM 46:1 NIV
"God is our refuge and strength, an ever-present help in trouble."

CHAPTER 17: WHEN YOU WALK ALONE IN YOUR DREAM...

RUTH 1:16 NIV
"Don't urge me to leave you or to turn back from you. Where you go I will go, and where you stay I will stay. Your people will be my people and your God my God."

ISAIAH 55:9 NKJV
" 'For as the heavens are higher than the earth, So are My ways higher than your ways, and My thoughts than your thoughts.' "

GET BACK UP! SCRIPTURES

CHAPTER 18: WHEN YOU HAVE AN EMOTIONAL WOUND...

GENESIS 50:19-20 NIV
"But Joseph said to them, 'Don't be afraid. Am I in the place of God? You intended to harm me, but God intended it for good to accomplish what is now being done, the saving of many lives.'"

CHAPTER 19: WHEN IT'S TIME TO REBUILD...

I SAMUEL 30:6 KJV
"And David was greatly distressed; for the people spake of stoning him, because the soul of all the people was grieved, every man for his sons and for his daughters: but David encouraged himself in the LORD his God."

CHAPTER 20: WHEN YOU FEEL UNWORTHY...

PSALM 51:10 NKJV
"Create in me a clean heart, O God, And renew a steadfast spirit in me."

CHAPTER 21: WHEN YOU CHANGE YOUR PERSPECTIVE...

LAMENTATIONS 3:22-23 NASB
"The LORD'S lovingkindnesses indeed never cease, For His compassions never fail. They are new every morning; Great is [His] faithfulness."

CHAPTER 22: WHEN YOU EXPERIENCE TRAUMA...

ECCLESIASTES 4:9-10 NIV
"Two are better than one, because they have a good return for their work: If one falls down, his friend can help him up.

But pity the man [or woman] who falls and has no one to help him [or her] up."

PSALMS 136:1 NIV
"Give thanks to the LORD, for [He] is good. His love endures forever."

ISAIAH 43:2 NIV
"When you pass through the waters, I will be with you; and when you pass through the rivers, they will not sweep over you. When you walk through the fire, you will not be burned; the flames will not set you ablaze."

CHAPTER 23: WHEN YOU NEED A COMEBACK...

ISAIAH 61:8 NLT
"For I, the LORD, love justice. I hate robbery and wrongdoing. I will faithfully reward my people for their suffering and make an everlasting covenant with them."

ROMANS 8:37 NIV
"No, in all these things we are more than conquerors through him who loved us."

2 COR. 2:14 NKJV
"Now thanks be to God who always leads us in triumph in Christ..."

MATTHEW 5:45 NKJV
"...that you may be sons of your Father in heaven; for He makes His sun rise on the evil and on the good, and sends rain on the just and on the unjust."

Chapter 24: When It's Time To Begin Again...

Isaiah 43:19 KJV

"Behold, I will do a new thing; now it shall spring forth; shall ye not know it? I will even make a way in the wilderness, and rivers in the desert."

Made in United States
Orlando, FL
12 November 2023